HUNGRY TOWN

TOM FITZMORRIS'S

HUNGRY TOWN

A CULINARY HISTORY OF NEW ORLEANS

The City Where Food Is Almost Everything

STEWART, TABORI & CHANG   NEW YORK

Published in 2010 by Stewart, Tabori & Chang
An imprint of ABRAMS

Text copyright © 2010 Tom Fitzmorris
Cover photographs © 2010 Jeff Elkins

Library of Congress Cataloguing-in-Publication Data

Fitzmorris, Tom, 1951-
Tom Fitzmorris's hungry town : a culinary history of New Orleans, the city where food is almost everything / Tom Fitzmorris.
    p. cm.
Includes bibliographical references and index.
ISBN 978-1-58479-801-9 (alk. paper)
1. Restaurants--Louisiana--New Orleans--History. 2. Cookery--Louisiana--New Orleans--History. 3. Fitzmorris, Tom, 1951- 4. Hurricane Katrina, 2005--Social aspects--Louisiana--New Orleans. I. Title.
TX907.3.L82F57 2010
641.59763'35--dc22

                          2009039995

Designer: Alissa Faden
Production Manager: Tina Cameron

The text of this book was composed in Sabon and Trade Gothic.

Printed and bound in the United States

10 9 8 7 6 5 4 3 2 1

Stewart, Tabori & Chang books are available at special discounts when purchased in quantity for premiums and promotions as well as fundraising or educational use. Special editions can also be created to specification. For details, contact specialsales@abramsbooks.com or the address below.

THE ART OF BOOKS SINCE 1949
115 West 18th Street
New York, NY 10011
www.abramsbooks.com

For the incomparable restaurateurs of New Orleans

CONTENTS

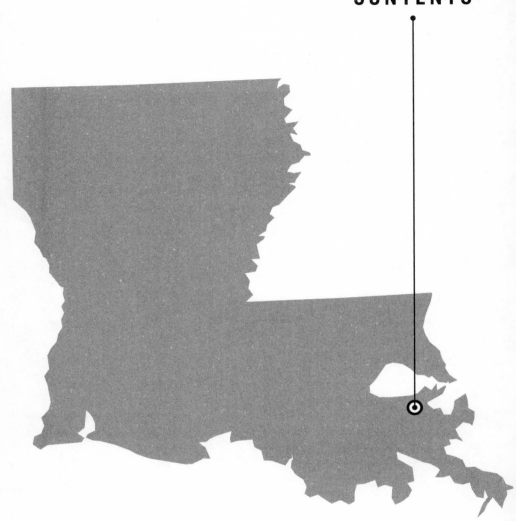

PART ONE

Doing What Comes Naturally

Commander's Palace. It took more than a year to repair the antebellum building after Katrina.

CHAPTER ONE

The Pleasures of Hard Times

EXPOSED TO THE ELEMENTS

New Orleans is like your first raw oyster. You must suspend your squeamishness and take it on its own terms to enjoy it. If you keep your distance, you'll never get it. If you go for it, though, you will be rewarded with the fulfillment of lust. Lust is an urge you need to have to live in this city successfully. Without lust, you're probably better off living somewhere else.

No matter what else you think or hear, the central lust in New Orleans is for eating. Passionate eaters recognize that about the city almost as soon as they arrive. The same way they do in Italy, France, and Spain, and for the same reasons.

Some people who love New Orleans might hesitate to credit something as quotidian as food with having so much magnetism. But not long ago some very convincing proof that food is almost everything was put before us. For New Orleanians, it was an extreme example of what we feel when we travel to another place and realize that the people there don't cook the way we do. We begin to itch to get back.

People who were living in New Orleans in the summer of 2005 will talk about what happened then for the rest of their lives. I was, and I will. Those of us who survived Hurricane Katrina (and many didn't; it was as bad as the television coverage made it look), those of us who love living in New Orleans, wondered what force possibly could pull our city and our lives back together.

To our surprise and delight, that force was provided in almost unbelievable measure by cooks, restaurants, gumbo, poor boy sandwiches, soft-shell crabs, and our love of eating together.

I should have known. I've spent my entire adult life eating, thinking about eating, writing about eating, and talking about eating. But every time I think about the role our unique culinary culture played after Katrina, I shake my head and grin.

My first inkling that something wonderful was about to happen came on October 12, 2005, with an e-mail from a reader of my Web site: "I saw in your newsletter that you're back in town. My wife and I have a reservation for eight o'clock at Restaurant August. She said that even though we don't really know you, you really ought to join us and our son as our guest. Please say yes!"

How could I say no? I'd just returned to New Orleans after six weeks of post-Katrina evacuation—my longest absence since I was born on Mardi Gras 1951. I was home alone while my wife and two teenage children remained evacuated in Washington, DC.

Downtown New Orleans was still a bizarre mix of familiarity and chaos. I parked my car on a sidewalk behind a fire hydrant on Gravier Street, just off Tchoupitoulas. The New Orleans Police Department was in disarray and wasn't paying the slightest attention to even flagrant parking violators. Across the street was Restaurant August, a primary contender for the title of best restaurant in town since it had opened in 2001.

I opened the door and pushed into the crowded bar. Every face I saw was familiar to me. Some were friends, some prominent New Orleanians, some both. Most of the men wore jackets and ties, as did I. The women were dressed beautifully.

For the next ten or fifteen minutes, we all gave each other the "Katrina hug." In those days, that's how we said, "My God! You're still alive!" Since well over a thousand people died as a result of the storm, the hug was given and received in earnest. After disengaging from it, we traded stories of our situations, knowing that we could go on for hours. Meanwhile, I scanned the room for my hosts. I saw three people I didn't recognize sitting in the corner of the bar. I figured it had to be them.

It was. They had a bottle of Veuve Clicquot open and a glass of it poured for me by the time I elbowed my way over to them. I gave these strangers the Katrina hug, and we began a (lengthy) dinner that will never fade from my memory.

I've had more than a few unforgettable dinners. I started writing about them in college, and I never quit. It became my life's work, distributed mostly in print and on the radio, but in practically every other medium too. What most engages me, in work and play, is the food of New Orleans. I love it passionately—as did these new friends who'd invited me to dinner. As compelling as our Katrina conversation was, they also wanted to talk about food.

We remained in the bar for more than an hour past our reservation time. When we were finally admitted to the dining room, another forty or fifty acquaintances needed the Katrina hug and a few words before I could sit down. After that, fifteen or twenty minutes more passed before a young woman wearing a Restaurant August T-shirt—not the standard uniform of the restaurant by a long shot—walked up, smiling and perspiring. "Welcome to August!" she said. "I'm Debbie, and I'll be your waitress tonight. I'm glad you have something to drink, because the next time you see me will be in about a half hour! Bye!"

We looked at one another and laughed. Octavio Mantilla, one of the owners of the restaurant, had warned us about this. Restaurant August typically has two dozen servers and busboys in the dining room and eleven cooks in the kitchen. That night, serving more customers than the restaurant could really hold, there were just three servers and two cooks; the whereabouts and fates of the absentees were still largely unknown.

One of the cooks was August's chef and co-owner, John Besh. A Marine sergeant in the first Gulf War, he was one of the two or three hottest chefs in town, with a growing national reputation. (He'd been on the cover of *Food & Wine* magazine, among others.) He's a good-looking, instantly likable guy and a well-trained, inspired restaurateur.

Besh returned to town soon after the storm, to find his restaurant had sustained little damage. That was a big relief not only to him, but also to people who liked him and his food. On CNN we'd all seen a much-replayed video of a burning building on the same block as August and wondered. During Besh's first days back, the city was still officially evacuated. A few people had never left town, especially in the French Quarter and the Warehouse District. But most of the people on the streets were military troops. His kitchen crippled by a lack of gas and water, Besh set up a propane burner and made pots of red beans and rice to feed these people, as well as anyone else who drifted by.

When they returned to their kitchens, Besh and other front-line chefs thought that any customers who showed up would be interested only in sustenance. While Besh cooked his beans, Scott Boswell, of the five-star Stella!, grilled hamburgers and sausages on a charcoal grill in his French Quarter courtyard. Bob Iacovone, of the four-star Cuvée, around the corner from August, made meat loaf.

When civilian customers began to return, however, they had different ideas. "What the hell is all this?" they wanted to know. "What about the gnocchi with the crabmeat and truffles? Where are the oysters and soft-shell crabs? Barbecue shrimp?"

The returning diners were also disappointed that the wine lists were attenuated. With power out for weeks, wine-storage-room temperatures (there are no cellars in New Orleans) climbed above a hundred degrees, popping corks from many bottles and cooking the rest. Millions of dollars in wine was lost in the first week of September 2005.

These were not the desires of callous people out of touch with the reality of the disaster. Eighty percent of the city was deeply flooded, and more than 100,000 houses were rendered uninhabitable. That affected nearly everybody. Many of the people who had lived in the flood zones were in a very bad fix, with no place to go, no food, no job, and no resources—but an equally large number of the homeless were in situations better described as extremely inconvenient than life-threatening. Quite a few of the gourmets at August, Stella!, and Cuvée were without a place to live. Some shared homes with friends. Others commuted into town from temporary quarters as far as a hundred miles away. Many of them had to deal with lost businesses and jobs. Yet there they were, dressed up, dining and drinking, smiling and laughing, almost as if nothing had happened.

Almost nobody in New Orleans escaped the crisis entirely. We were all concerned about the condition and future of the city, which at the very least was cause for alarm. Every level of government, local to federal, was dissolving in a swamp of incompetence and shifting blame. But, by God, if we could go out to dinner and find that the essence of living in New Orleans—this eating and drinking like nobody in the world does the way we do—was still there . . . well, then, it might be possible to go on.

So, we went on. And we ate. We ate in grand restaurants like August if that's what we needed to do to be convinced that the food infrastructure was still sound. Or we ate in raffish old poor boy shops like Mother's, a block away. Or in our own kitchens (or those of the people who were letting us stay with them), cooking our own red beans and rice, and gumbo. We cooked and ate not just to fill our stomachs, but to live the New Orleans life, eating and drinking with relieved abandon.

The urgent return to New Orleans food cut across all of society's imaginary lines. Rich to poor, black to white, comfortable to homeless. Most New Orleanians ate the military MREs (meals ready to eat) the FEMA folks vouchsafed us—if only until we could get our hands on some shrimp, a pan, and some kind of cookstove.

Every restaurant that found enough employees (and that was their most vexing problem) was overflowing with customers. And they didn't seem to care how long the wait was for a table or how limited the menu. They'd just get a drink and get back to telling Katrina tales. People had a lot of time on their hands; many were on furlough from their jobs and had nothing much else to do. Money didn't seem to be a problem; insurance was coming in, and everybody got a $2,000 check from FEMA. *Laissez le bon temps rouler!*

THE COUNTER CLICKS

I had an inkling things would go this way about three weeks before. At that time, large sections of the city were still flooded, and a second enormous hurricane—what a sick joke that was!—saw the town reevacuated. I was holed up in a basement in rural Maryland, the guest of an elderly semirelative, who had dial-up Internet service and only one phone; I couldn't get online until after she went to bed. In one night's flood of e-mail I came across what seemed an absurd question: "Would you send me a list of all the New Orleans restaurants open right now?"

"Are you kidding?" I wrote back. "The whole city is shut down. People aren't even supposed to be there. The number of restaurants open in New Orleans is zero!"

Three more people asked the same question the next night. And more each night after. I figured I'd better check around. Battling through the badly compromised New Orleans phone system, I found out that twenty-two restaurants were somehow back in business. Most were outside the city proper, but a few in the French Quarter and up Magazine Street had opened, too. I posted the list on my Web site and directed the ever-increasing number of inquirers there. Day after day, I added restaurants to the list as I found out about them.

That list—which I called the New Orleans Restaurant Index, and still update daily—captured more attention than anything else I'd ever done. My count of open restaurants is widely quoted in the national and local media and even in mayoral speeches. The city's main tourism bureau gave me its "Hero Award" for it.

And today the Index provides one statistic that never fails to astound: New Orleans has substantially more restaurants now than it did before the hurricane. It seems hard to believe. Unless, of course, you're one of those who understands what a hungry town New Orleans is.

DELICIOUS GRAVITY

But back to that dinner at Restaurant August. My new friends and I began our dinner with an *amuse-bouche* from the chef—seared foie gras. Then, fried Florida oysters. (I would, with amazement and lust, eat my first post-storm Louisiana raw oysters a few days later.) Next, the misleadingly named, outrageously over-the-top dish we call barbecue shrimp in New Orleans. John Besh does a particularly good version of them with enormous Louisiana shrimp.

The entrées included mussels with fries, filet mignon with an intense demi-glace sauce, and buttery almond-crusted sautéed sheepshead (an underrated Gulf fish), topped with jumbo lump Louisiana crabmeat. It was all as marvelous as it would have been before the storm. Only two concessions had to be made to the stresses of the moment: We had to use some paper napkins and plastic plates (although most of the meal was on china, with silverware). And the French fries were frozen (the produce truck carrying the fresh potatoes had rolled over a particularly sharp piece of debris—one of millions strewn on the streets—and didn't make it).

As we did with the other deviations from the norm that we had come to expect in our lives, we laughed these off. How could they diminish the joy of a dinner like this? Or the knowledge that we could find other places to do it again tomorrow? Nobody I saw leaving Restaurant August that night was sporting anything less than a happy countenance.

The people who never had much of a romance with the city in the first place saw nothing but a shocking mess. To them, the idea that food could possibly compensate for the disadvantages of living in that morass was ridiculous. And maybe they're right. In addition to dangerous hurricanes and precarious levees, New Orleanians must battle with a chronically sluggish economy, a high crime rate, and embarrassingly poor public education. The disenchanted citizens made a good case for leaving forever, and many of them did.

Unfortunately for me, my wife Mary Ann, my son Jude, and my daughter Mary Leigh joined this justifiably disdainful group. They didn't want to come back from Washington. Jude never really did. What began as a temporary enrollment in a boarding school there became permanent. The Marys came back home for a few months but went back to Washington for many more. They didn't return permanently to our (undamaged) rural home near Abita Springs until the summer of 2007. And then, begrudgingly.

Although they're thankful I make a living at it, they can't understand the delight I take in my work. It requires me to live in New Orleans to pursue it; that diminishes most of its appeal for them. But not for me. I can't imagine living without my peculiar work. Or living anywhere but New Orleans. Even though, frankly, in the months following Hurricane Katrina I had no idea what value such a frothy, inessential pursuit could have in the distressed city.

Which brings up the question everybody asks me: "How did you get a job like that?" The dialogue stops short until I answer. So I'll get that out of the way in the next chapter.

KATRINA TIMETABLE

From a Culinary Perspective

People living in the city of New Orleans, most of its suburbs, and the Mississippi Gulf Coast are ordered to evacuate as the storm grows to an almost unimaginable size, with Category 5 winds. Every restaurant in the New Orleans area closes, as highways fill with escaping citizens.

A nearly complete breakdown of federal, state, local, and private services brings chaos, looting, and the stranding of thousands of people. Deaths are in the hundreds. Despite this, many people continue to live in the French Quarter and elsewhere on the high ground near the river. Some chefs and restaurateurs already have emergency cooking centers to feed first responders.

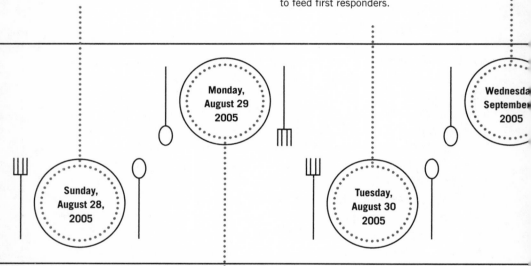

Sunday, August 28, 2005

Monday, August 29 2005

Tuesday, August 30 2005

Wednesda September 2005

Katrina makes landfall at Category 4 strength, with a storm surge that completely submerges Plaquemines Parish before slamming into the Mississippi Gulf Coast. Winds in excess of a hundred miles per hour are felt throughout the New Orleans area. The wind damage is widespread and very serious. But a worse disaster begins when levees break at several points on the canals leading to the swollen Lake Pontchartrain. During the next two days, the water deepens, until more than 80 percent of the city is flooded—to a depth of more than ten feet in many large areas. It will take more than three weeks to pump all the water out.

•• The five-star Dakota Restaurant opens in the North Shore suburb of Covington, which had heavy wind damage but no flooding. It is the first major restaurant in the New Orleans area to resume some semblance of normal service. The public water supply in New Orleans is considered unsafe, and gas and electricity are almost entirely out. Nevertheless, some restaurants in New Orleans proper return, in emergency mode. Top chefs Paul Prudhomme, John Besh, Horst Pfeifer, Scott Boswell, Andrea Apuzzo, and others are cooking and serving whatever they can. Emeril Lagasse is organizing other superstar chefs to host dinners around the country to raise millions of dollars to help New Orleans. Drago's, the major seafood restaurant in the suburb of Metairie, begins giving food to anyone who comes to its doors. It will eventually serve 77,000 free meals.

Mr. B's reopens after the very difficult repair of its storm damage. It brings the number of restaurants open in the New Orleans area to 809—the same number open the day before the Katrina evacuation.

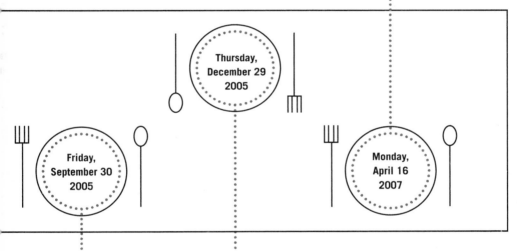

Ralph Brennan opens Bacco and Red Fish Grill in the French Quarter for nearly full service, even though the public water supply is still regarded as being undrinkable. Bottled water is used for everything. All plates and utensils are disposable. From this experience, the State Department of Health creates guidelines for allowing restaurants to reopen. Restaurants begin to open at the rate of several per day. Even though most residents are still evacuated, restaurant staffs are sparse, and food is difficult to obtain, every open restaurant does all-time-record business.

Antoine's reopens. America's oldest continuously operating restaurant, opened in 1840 by the family that still owns it today, Antoine's main building was so heavily damaged by the storm that it nearly collapsed. Three days later, Galatoire's—widely considered the most important of the grand old restaurants—opens its doors to a full house.

My Katrina Disaster

I was very lucky during Hurricane Katrina. My house was undamaged, and I didn't miss one week's pay. Then, afterward, my New Orleans Menu *newsletter actually became much more successful than it had been before the hurricane. I did suffer one great loss, however. My office was right behind the Superdome and flooded about four and a half feet deep. Everything in it was destroyed. Thirty years' worth of photographs, including the negatives. Boxes and boxes of menus from the restaurants I had visited over the years. And the magazines and newspapers that had published my work. Having that stuff would have improved this book. But, compared with what happened to many other Orleanians, I hesitate to complain.*

Fortunately, I lost none of my article archives from 1984 onward, since they were all well backed-up on computers. And, in an unbelievable stroke of luck, one of the subscribers to The New Orleans Menu *had every single issue ever published, from 1977 onward. She was about to throw them all away, but she sent them to me instead.*

Crabmeat Berdou

Long before it closed in the 1990s, Berdou's was in a time-warp, operating in the style of a much older restaurant. This dish was a favored specialty, and I get requests for it regularly. George Berdou himself demonstrated the dish on my television show; it was a keeper. It will appeal especially to garlic lovers.

Béchamel	Crabmeat Mixture
4 Tbs. butter	1 stick butter
3 Tbs. flour	½ cup green onions, chopped
1 cup milk, warmed	½ cup mushrooms, sliced
½ tsp. salt	1 Tbs. garlic, chopped
	Pinch cayenne
	½ cup sherry
	1 lb. lump crabmeat

Preheat the broiler with the rack about four inches below the heat.

1. Prepare the béchamel. Heat the four tablespoons butter in a saucepan until it bubbles. Stir in the flour to make a blond roux; don't allow it to brown. Whisk in the milk over low heat, until the sauce thickens. Add the salt, and keep warm.

2. In a second saucepan, heat the stick of butter until it bubbles, add the green onions, mushrooms, garlic, and cayenne, and sauté until the mushrooms are tender. Add the sherry, and bring to a boil. Lower the heat, and cook until all the liquid is absorbed.

3. Carefully add the lump crabmeat, agitating the pan to combine with the rest of the ingredients, so as not to break the lumps. Divide the mixture onto ovenproof serving plates: six to eight for appetizers, four for entrees.

4. Nap two or three tablespoons of the béchamel for appetizers, or a generous quarter cup for entrees. Put the plates into the hot broiler for about a minute. Serve immediately, warning guests that the plates are hot.

MAKES SIX TO EIGHT APPETIZERS OR FOUR ENTRÉES.

A good, gravy-laden, sloppy roast beef poor boy, the dish that turned me on to lustful eating.

CHAPTER TWO

How I Got This Job: A Lucky Coincidence of Interests

THE POOR BOY

Before I ever thought out what I'd do for a living, I knew that I liked investigating the food I ate more thoroughly than most other people I knew or read about. The realization came courtesy of Uncle Billy—my *parran*. That's what you call your godfather if you come from a French-speaking New Orleans family, as I do. He was a longshoreman, a solid, salt-of-the-earth guy, gregarious and always laughing. He hung out and drank beer with his buddies at Clarence and Lefty's, one of scores of neighborhood bars scattered throughout the city. In those days, most of them served food, too. One night when I was eight or nine years old, Uncle Billy was stuck with me for the evening. He took me along to Clarence and Lefty's. He thought I was too skinny, and he had a plan for fixing that. He sat me down at a table and said, "Here's what you're going to eat for supper, Tommy!" A motherly waitress set a roast beef poor boy in front of me; it was my first encounter with the classic New Orleans sandwich. A foot-long piece of French bread, stuffed with thickly sliced beef round, drooling with brown gravy. I was a picky eater, and this wasn't my kind of thing. But I couldn't say no to Uncle Billy, who was a much tougher guy than, say, my dad.

I picked up the enormous sandwich and took a bite. Uncle Billy beamed. "You gonna like that!" he said, and returned to the bar. I was no stranger to delicious food. My mother was legendary in her family as a great Creole cook. But that was everyday food for me. This was something else again. The crisp, light bread . . . the meaty, intense gravy . . . the mayonnaise and tomatoes and pickles . . . it all came together in one irresistible eat.

Uncle Billy checked back after a few minutes. He looked angry. "What did you do with that poor boy?" he demanded.

"I ate it!" I said. "It was good!"

His face returned to its kinder squinty grin. "Yeah? You want another one?" He surely was kidding. But I told him that I did.

Nobody can eat two roast beef poor boys from a New Orleans neighborhood bar. But I put a good dent in the second one. Those sandwiches in that old dump left me with a taste memory that still lingers as vividly as anything. One thing I knew from that moment: Very few dishes in the world are as delicious as a well-made New Orleans roast beef poor boy.

And then, taking a wider view, I also knew that there had to be plenty more new good things to eat out there.

RADIO PLAYBOY

At the same time that I discovered the poor boy, another strong interest was forming in my mind; I never imagined the two would merge into a career. It started in a tree. I sat in it, listening to a transistor radio. It was 1962, and the two New Orleans rock stations were engaged in an epic battle that wound up changing the sound of radio nationwide. The two inventors of Top Forty radio each owned radio stations in New Orleans—the only city where they competed against each other. They threw their best disc jockeys, jingles, and formats into the battle as they played pre-Beatles rock music.

Young teenagers like me were their target audience; I hardly ever took the earphones off. After one particularly funny burst of deejay patter, I jumped down from the tree and went inside to tell my dad the news: "I know what I'm going to be when I grow up! A radio disc jockey!"

He laughed. "You can't do that. Those guys are just a bunch of playboys!"

While that shut my mouth, I was sure of my new goal, and I thought about my dad's advice. Okay, then, step one: Become a playboy.

But what, I wondered, does a playboy do? The answer came from a now-defunct comic strip called *Steve Roper*. The title character was a magazine reporter who lived a life of bullet-dodging adventure, but with an understated, civilized personal style. In the adventure of the moment, Roper's editor had hired a glamorous new fashion writer and asked Roper to show her around town. She was dubious about Roper—particularly when the taxi taking them to dinner dropped them in front of a warehouse in a rough neighborhood.

Roper knocked on the battered door; a tuxedoed maître d' opened it. "Ah, Mr. Roper! Your table is ready and your Champagne is chilled. We have your favorite cut of venison tonight. Please come in!" Roper and the fashion reporter sat down to what, at the end of the repast, she described as the most spectacular dinner of her life.

"How did you find this place, and why is it hidden?" she asked.

"The chef doesn't want everybody to know about it," Roper said. "Only people who appreciate the best."

Wow! If anything in the world were worth knowing, I thought, it would be something like that. People would listen if a radio playboy talked about such things on the air.

KNOWING WHAT'S GOOD

A few years later, on my high school senior trip, my classmates and I visited Washington, DC, and New York City. This would be the point in most food writers' memoirs when they experience a revelation in taste. For me, it was the other way around. We went to some pretty good restaurants, for teenagers. But my fellow travelers and I agreed that nobody up there seemed to know what was good. No roast beef poor boys—anywhere? No gumbo? No fried oysters? What, were these people nuts? We couldn't wait to get back home and eat real food again.

Not long before, Craig Claiborne had begun writing what is generally acknowledged as the first real restaurant review column in America, for *The New York Times*. I wonder what would have happened if I had read it then. I suspect it would have been another *Steve Roper*-type revelation.

That eye-opener came two and a half years later. I remember

the moment vividly. My buddy Chris Christopher and I were walking across the campus of what is now called the University of New Orleans (UNO). We were nineteen and had just left home to rent a house with some other guys. As we walked, Chris read out of a book bits he found intriguing and hilarious. The author was Richard Collin, one of our history professors. He'd just published the latest in Simon and Schuster's *Underground Gourmet* series, guides to inexpensive, unpretentious, and oftentimes ethnic restaurants. But *The New Orleans Underground Gourmet* took a different tack from those in other cities. Since most restaurants in New Orleans were (and are) inexpensive, unpretentious, and, in their local way, ethnic, Collin's book covered the city's entire restaurant scene—from Buster Holmes, with its platters of beans for fifty cents, to Galatoire's and LeRuth's, the best New Orleans restaurants of their day.

His wasn't the first New Orleans restaurant guide. But Collin was the first to say, in print, that some restaurants were far better than others. That some were nowhere near as fine as their reputations. And—most interesting to us college students—that some of the best food in town could be found in some of the least known, cheapest places.

Collin wrote in high contrasts. If he liked a restaurant or a dish, he made it sound as if it lifted the diner to Valhalla. If he didn't, he could be devastatingly derisive. Lines like "The food is nothing to write home about, although you might have time in the long pauses between courses" and "It would be a bad deal if it were free" raised eyebrows—especially when applied to famous, allegedly excellent establishments.

Collin's book altered the food consciousness of New Orleans residents. Dramatically. And that is saying something, given how much thought we always gave to what we ate. We were convinced that our city was the home of some of the country's best food. But few of us had any idea how broad the culinary world in New Orleans really was. Inspired by Collin's reviews, we began, avidly, to try new eateries and dishes.

Restaurateurs were suspicious of Collin. He forced them, through his readers, to rethink their comfortable games. They didn't like to have to do that. Some fought him, trying hard not to change, trying to convince people that their food really was as good as they said it was. But many more New Orleans diners had now tasted of the Tree of Good and Bad, and found new options they hadn't known they had. It was the start of a sweeping, overdue improvement in the local restaurant scene.

I had grown up eating great food, but only at home. My family never went to restaurants—not even little neighborhood places. But I made up for that—quickly. By my late teens I was already in the habit of dining in restaurants. I loved everything about the experience. Like most people, though, my universe was limited to a small number of restaurants serving familiar food. What I learned from reading Collin jazzed me up. And became an obsession. This mix of familiar and unknown pleasures was deeply alluring. Reading his book was like looking through a telescope for the first time.

I embarked on a program of restaurant adventures. It spiraled out from neighborhood cafés and poor boy shops to soul food restaurants in mostly black neighborhoods. (I was struck by how similar the cooking there was to my mother's.) Then I moved up to bistros and ethnic restaurants, all new to me. I ate food I would never have considered trying before. My palate became omnivorous.

That took fortitude at times. Once a buddy accused me of not being much of a gourmet, because I didn't eat raw oysters. He shamed me into going to Felix's Oyster Bar to lose my virginity. It was unpleasant. It required real determination to eat the half dozen large bivalves on the marble-topped bar before me. I ate too many crackers and too much ketchup-and-horseradish sauce, trying to buffer the cold, unique flavor and mouthfeel of the oysters. I was glad when the last one was down.

But a funny thing happened a few days later. I was suddenly struck with a desire to eat more oysters. This time, I knocked back a dozen. I was soon convinced—as I still am—that oysters are the most delicious of all seafoods.

It took a while to break down other barriers, too. Because I've always spent more time working than I should (to the detriment of my grades, back then), I had the money to go to Antoine's, Galatoire's, Brennan's, LeRuth's, and the other grand restaurants in town, with their numerous Collin stars. But I had neither the confidence to go, nor friends with matching funds. Instead, my introduction to haute cuisine came from an unexpected source.

A Restaurant Discovery

In 1972, I quit the job I'd had since I was twelve working in a grocery store to take a job with *Figaro*, a new alternative weekly newspaper, begun by James K. Glassman. (Now a well-known political and economics writer in Washington, DC, Glassman had married a New Orleans woman and was launching his career in town.) I was already writing movie, theater, and music reviews for the *Driftwood*, UNO's campus newspaper. Originally, my job at the *Driftwood* was as its editorial cartoonist. When the fall semester began, though, a new editor cleaned house. He told me his friend would take over my cartoonist gig—and that I was, like, fired. Not wanting to give up the clubhouse privileges that accrue to newspaper staff, I begged to stay on to write feature articles.

"Like what?" he asked.

I had no ideas prepared, but I thought fast. "Do you know about the Flambeau Room?" I asked, quite sure that he didn't. The Flambeau Room was a white-tablecloth restaurant in the student center, patronized mostly by faculty but open to anyone. It had waiters and waitresses, bone china, and silverware. The manager was Peter Sclafani, Jr., the son of one of the city's most celebrated Italian chefs. The chef was Leon Ricard, who had spent a few years at Brennan's; the Brennans liked him enough to send him to the Cordon Bleu.

The Flambeau Room served slightly scaled-back versions of Brennan's food, at absurdly low prices. A lunch of turtle soup, chicken Clemenceau, and caramel custard went for $1.50. That was lower than the price of a hamburger, fries, and a Coke in the snack bar next door. I knew a good deal when I saw one, and I ate in the Flambeau Room every day. There I tasted oysters Bienville, shrimp rémoulade, eggs Sardou, redfish court bouillon, filet mignon marchand de vin, and dozens of other classic French-Creole dishes for the first time. The chef liked to use béarnaise sauce, which I found astonishingly delicious.

Top New Orleans Restaurants, 1970

This is how the New Orleans restaurant scene stacked up when I became conscious of it, at age nineteen. The ratings are those of Richard Collin in *The New Orleans Underground Gourmet*, the first set of restaurant ratings ever published in New Orleans. The bolded restaurants are still open as of 2010. The top restaurants for various years appear elsewhere in this book. More about these restaurants is available online: http://www.nomenu.com/HistoricalRatings

★★★★ **FOUR STARS** ★★★★
(the maximum rating)

Galatoire's
LeRuth's

★★★ **THREE STARS** ★★★

Acme Oyster House
Andrew Jackson
Antoine's
Barataria Tavern
Brennan's
Caribbean Room
Chez Helene
Christopher Blake's
Commander's Palace
Crescent City Steak House
Elmwood Plantation
España
Gin's Mee Hong
Mosca's
Pascal's Manale
Ristorante Tre Fontane

"Sure," said the new editor. "Write about that."

My piece ran in the *Driftwood* on September 1, 1972. It was unambiguously a review. I held forth on what I thought was great and what could be better. I based my decrees purely on the impressions of my naive palate. Despite that, the article was received as credible. The editor, in the only smart move he ever made (he was gone by the spring semester), told me I ought to write a weekly column about other places to eat on- and off-campus.

That began the column I write every week to this day. And my career as a restaurant critic and food writer. It set a pattern of impecuniousness, too. The cost of the meals I reviewed wasn't reimbursed by the *Driftwood*. In fact, I have yet to find an employer willing to cover my expenses, which run far into five figures every year. While that makes for a significant tax deduction, it remains the one undeniable drawback of my work. Writing restaurant reviews came with other benefits, though. Women thought it was a cool thing for a guy to do. Cooler still if the guy invited her along to partake in the review meals. Without realizing it, I had followed in the footsteps of Steve Roper—if rather far behind him. Not a playboy, but with some worldliness. Perhaps even enough to become a voice on the radio. That was still my primary goal, and my college major.

My father never understood any of this, and he kept asking when I'd get a real job.

A REAL JOB

In 1974, the month I graduated from college, I published my first restaurant column i.. *New Orleans* magazine, a slick, inoffensive monthly. It paid well (no expense account, though) and had some cachet. I must have made an impression on the publisher, Joe David III, because after four months he offered me the job of editor in chief.

I was twenty-three. Although working with Glassman at *Figaro* had given me confidence in my ability to build a publication, I have to admit now that I was in over my head. Fortunately, a cadre of talented freelance writers and artists were always at my door, and we wound up putting out a product that doesn't embarrass me to peruse all these years later.

I discovered early on at *New Orleans* magazine that our local audience knew no limits when it came to articles about eating. They devoured the material much more avidly than they did traditional food writing, which was mostly about cooking. Cooking and eating are related, but they're not the same thing. For every person who likes to cook, ten or a hundred or a thousand people like to eat. So the number of magazine pages we devoted to restaurants tripled—at least. I wrote most of the articles myself. The other writers thought I was overdoing it, but the advertising staff was very pleased. A slick magazine with heavy food coverage attracts a lot of restaurant advertising.

A highlight of my time at the magazine was my cover story for the December 1975 issue. I challenged a chef to mount the grandest imaginable New Orleans–style Christmas dinner. Christopher Blake, a flamboyant character with a history of cooking great food, accepted with alacrity. Richard Collin had awarded three out of a possible four stars to Chris's short-lived eponymous restaurant; the mayor had named Chris "Gourmet Laureate of New Orleans," whatever that means.

To keep his projects going, Chris spent a lot of time looking for benefactors. His patron at the time was Daniel Fusilier, a Cajun gourmet and bon vivant. Fusilier agreed to host the *New Orleans* magazine Christmas dinner in his Uptown home. He gave Chris a blank check for the food and wine, and Chris used it to the fullest extent, with great delight.

On October 3, 1975 (we had a long lead time at the magazine), it was Christmas at Fusilier's place. Chris was a whirlwind in the kitchen. Fusilier, me, and seven others, none of whom I knew, filled the dining room. All but one of them became longtime friends. Three—Marc Winston, Marcelle Bienvenu, and Max Zander—would become key people in my life years later.

The dinner was a blend of New Orleans and French classics, involving some exotic ingredients. Chris flew in salmon trout from the Northwest, at a time when nobody in New Orleans ever ate fresh salmon of any kind. With so many great local fish species in New Orleans, importing fish by air seemed a far-out idea. But he'd made some connection with the Lummi Nation, and there the fish was. Through some other schmooze he acquired a pound of beluga caviar. To top it off, Marti's Restaurant sent over not only raw oysters but a shucker to open them for us.

The presence of Max Zander—who managed the city's dominant fine-wine distributorship—meant that Chris's cooking was balanced with an extraordinary collection of wines, all but one of them French, from the loftiest sources. The wine alone would put several

The *New Orleans* magazine Christmas Dinner, 1975

Here is the menu for the dinner Christopher Blake cooked for ten people. The actual menus were individually inscribed by a talented calligrapher working in several colors.

Fresh Beluga Caviar Mousse
Champagne Rene Lalou 1966

Raw Oysters on the Half Shell
Barton & Guestier Muscadet 1972

Petite Marmite of Chicken, Beef, and Vegetables
Sherry La Ina Pedro Domeque

Salmon Trout with Fumet and Truffles
Le Reine Pedaque Montrachet 1969

Sorbet au Citron
Calvados

Vol-au-Vent of Veal Sweetbreads and Duck Breast
Financiere with Soufflée of Mirlitons
Chateau La Mission Haut-Brion 1962
Chateau Montrose 1962

Salade Verte

Buche de Noel
Chateau d'Yquem 1967

Assortment of Cheeses and Fresh Fruits

Café Filtre

Cognac Bisquit

This dinner would be considered extravagant today; it was almost unimaginable then. In 1975, there were no degustation menus or wine dinners in restaurants. To have a dinner like this, you had to be a member of a private gourmet society, like the Chaine des Rotisseurs.

exclamation points behind this dinner today.

Chris didn't miss a step. The oysters, caviar, and Champagne would have made Steve Roper grin. The salmon trout surprised everybody with its intense goodness. The vol-au-vent of sweetbreads was the sort of thing you'd fly to Paris to find again. It was a sybaritic evening, lasting into the wee hours. The company could hardly have been better. Chris and his companion, Rock, were bon vivants of the highest order; Dan Fusilier and Marcelle Bienvenu were not only celebratory, but Cajuns—and nobody enjoys a good feed more than a Cajun does; Max Zander had a lifetime of stories to tell about other dinners and other wines.

It made a delicious cover story for the magazine. I took it to extremes, with a gatefold center spread and lots of color photographs. After that, whenever anyone asked me what I knew about gourmet dining, I just pulled out a copy of the issue and said, "Well, I did this dinner."

FOOD ALL OVER THE RADIO

My food writing was getting somewhere. But I still viewed that as secondary to my primary career goal in broadcasting. In 1975, I finally scored a regular on-air gig, a daily restaurant review on the city's leading news-talk station, WGSO. It did not surprise me when it grabbed much more attention than all my work in print had. And it brought many new readers to my column.

It was good timing, too, because *New Orleans* magazine was bought out from under me in 1977. The new owner wanted a different magazine from the one I produced, and I found myself without a steady job for the first time since I was twelve. Interviews locally didn't go well; many potential employers were deterred by the fact that anything they had for me would be a huge comedown from the editorship of *New Orleans* magazine. Really, what a normal person would have done was to scout around in bigger markets.

But I couldn't imagine leaving New Orleans or its food. Until something came along, I thought I'd start a publication of my own. *The New Orleans Menu* began as a four-page newsletter full of restaurant reviews, promoted on my radio shows. It did better than I expected, getting a few thousand paid subscribers and growing into a forty-page magazine. One of the first subscribers was David Kleck, an advertising man and gourmet. He was the first person I ever met who'd eaten sushi. He sent a note along with his ten-dollar subscription check: "Excellent idea. Please keep it distinctly New Orleans." I still follow that advice.

With lots of time on my hands, I hung around the radio station until somebody decided it would be a good idea to have me host a live talk show. At the time, the station's hosts played music and took phone calls, too—a combination then common but soon phased out. I could finally satisfy my desire to be a disc jockey—something I tired of quickly. My show went all talk after a few months. It expanded to four hours a day, five days a week by 1979, and covered everything under the sun. I found, however, that I could always perk up a slow show by talking about restaurants or cooking. The audience for that discussion seemed insatiable. The program director, on the other hand, disapproved. He didn't view food as a worthwhile topic—a stance I still encounter among the corporate managers at my present station.

What allowed me to gainsay these doubters was the show's appeal to restaurant and food sponsors. Although my audiences have never been enormous, everybody who listens is enthusiastic about food. Sponsors saw results. My show was and is very easy to sell. And the moment was right. The most exciting time in the history of the New Orleans restaurant business was just beginning.

Roast Beef Poor Boys

The poor boy sandwich is one of the essential flavors of New Orleans, and the roast beef is the king of the poor boys. The sandwich was invented in the mid-1920s, during a streetcar strike. Bennie and Clovis Martin, the owners of a busy restaurant on the corner of Touro and St. Claude, helped the "poor boys" on the picket lines by making a sandwich, on French bread, of roast beef gravy and all the little bits of beef that came with it. It was filling and delicious, and at a nickel per sandwich, affordable. After the strike was over, sliced beef was added to the gravy, and the price went up to a lofty dime. All that was left was for the John Gendusa Bakery to devise an extra long loaf of French bread, uniform in cross section, specifically for making poor boys. The sandwich—soon stuffed not only with roast beef but with just about anything else you can imagine—became so popular that the restaurant renamed itself Martin's Poor Boy Restaurant (not *po-boy*, although that has become the more common spelling in New Orleans).

Making roast beef for poor boys is more about making gravy than roasting beef. Inside round seems to taste best, but some cooks like eye of round or even rib eyes. It's best to cook the beef the day before, because it will throw off lots of good juices for the gravy, and the cold beef will be easier to slice. You can keep the gravy in a well-sealed container in the refrigerator for a few weeks, or freeze it for even longer storage.

The most critical step in making a roast beef poor boy is to put the whole assembled sandwich into a hot oven for two or three minutes before serving. The flavor and aroma of the toasted French bread doubles the goodness.

The recipe follows.

Roast Beef Poor Boys

4 to 6 lbs. inside round of beef, trimmed
Salt and pepper
2 Tbs. vegetable oil
1 large onion, quartered
4 ribs celery, cut up
1 garlic clove, peeled and cut in half
2 medium carrots, cut up
2 bay leaves
½ tsp. thyme
½ tsp. marjoram
¼ tsp. black peppercorns
1 to 3 Tbs. all-purpose flour
1 Tbs. Worcestershire sauce
3 loaves poor boy bread (available only in New Orleans, unfortunately),
   or 6 French baguettes
1 head lettuce, shredded coarsely
8 tomatoes, sliced thinly
Dill pickle slices
Mayonnaise

Preheat oven to 325 degrees.

1. Season the beef with salt and pepper. Heat the oil over medium-high heat in a Dutch oven or kettle big enough to hold the beef round, and brown the beef on all sides.

2. Remove the beef from the kettle and add the onion, celery, garlic, and carrots. Cook the vegetables until the onions brown a bit. Return the roast to the pot and fill the pot about a third of the full with water. Add the bay leaves, thyme, marjoram, and peppercorns. Cover the pot and put it into the preheated oven. Cook for four to six hours, turning the roast and adding more water every hour or so. The water level should slowly drop, but don't let it get less than about three inches deep. The beef is ready when a meat thermometer pushed into the center reads 160 degrees.

3. Remove the roast from the pot and place in a pan deep enough to

catch all the juices that run out as it cools. If you're cooking a day ahead (recommended), wrap the beef and refrigerate it as soon as it cools to just warm to the touch. If you're serving it that day, wait at least an hour before slicing.

4. Meanwhile, strain the solids from the stock in the pot. Bring the stock to a simmer. Add the juices that run from the roast, as well as the crumbs of beef that fall off as you slice it. Skim off the fat that rises to the surface, and cook stock until its consistency is that of a light gravy. (The gravy, like the beef, benefits from being made a day ahead and cooling in the refrigerator.)

5. When you're ready to make the sandwiches, preheat the oven to 400 degrees. Bring the gravy to a simmer, and whisk in the flour (but only if the gravy appears to need thickening). Add salt, pepper, and Worcestershire to taste.

6. Slice the roast beef as thinly as possible, and lay slices over bread to taste, with lettuce, tomatoes, pickles, and mayonnaise. Spoon on all the gravy the sandwich can hold. After assembling, put the sandwich into a 400-degree oven for about a minute to toast the bread.

MAKES TWELVE TO EIGHTEEN POOR BOYS.

My radio show microphone, with the station's original 1925 call letters.

CHAPTER THREE

New Orleans Learns to Eat All Over Again

OUR EYES ARE OPENED

A caller to my radio show one day demanded to know, "Just when did New Orleans become gourmet?" The way he said the word *gourmet* made it clear that he didn't think of it as a positive thing.

"New Orleans has always been a gourmet town!" I told him.

"No, it hasn't," he insisted. "We always had good food. You go to anybody's house or any corner joint, and you get good food. If you don't get good food, you think there must be something wrong with the cook. But now people make a big deal about it and about all those restaurants that charge you an arm and a leg for a bowl of gumbo that I can make better than they do!"

It was a good point, and it fired up the rest of the show. Most people agreed that New Orleans food was at its best when it was its honest, unassuming self. When it posed as gourmet, it was suspect.

Few other places in the America of 1981 could have kept up that conversation for more than a few minutes. The people calling my show kept after it for days. Maybe weeks.

That's because we had so much material. Unlike most American cities, New Orleans laid claim to a fully developed, distinctive regional cuisine at least a century old. In the 1880s, the first (and quite thick already) cookbooks about Creole cooking appeared. Those books didn't start any trends. They simply reported on the unique cooking and eating that was already part of day-to-day life in New Orleans.

New Orleans, it has often been said, is the most European of American cities. That's certainly true in the food department. As in

Europe, pleasurable eating is assumed. When something has gone wrong and it's not there, *then* it's a subject of conversation. Or maybe when it's time to compliment the cook—but sometimes not even then.

So here we were on the radio, trying to decide when we became consciously aware of just how good our food was. And whether this was a good or a bad thing.

Many theories were advanced. One of my favorites was this: "New Orleans went gourmet when Galatoire's got rid of those tiny wine glasses that the waiters would fill to the top." I knew exactly the glasses he was talking about. They were still in use in a few unreconstructed restaurants around town. He felt the change was an improvement. Others noted the opening of this or that restaurant as the dawning of the self-conscious gourmet era. A few pointed to the publication of *The Underground Gourmet*. One said the era began when the twenty-five-cent martini disappeared from Brennan's. (If that's what started it, then what are we to make of the widespread return of the two-bit martini in the 2000s?)

As for me, I know exactly when New Orleans stopped taking its food culture for granted and began instead to think about, talk about, and celebrate it all the time: July 17, 1979. On that hot evening, on my way to dinner somewhere in the French Quarter, I noticed activity inside a defunct restaurant on the corner of Royal and Iberville. I looked in and saw familiar faces. Ella and Dick Brennan and their executive chef Paul Prudhomme were standing inside a fully furnished dining room, checking things out. Ella saw my face and motioned me to the side door.

"You've got to see this!" she said, hustling me into the kitchen. "We're opening a new restaurant here in three days. It's going to be something different."

I followed her through the kitchen, in the middle of which was a big open-pit grill. "We're going to grill fish over burning hickory wood," she said. "Steaks and whatever else the chef wants, too. Over there, we're going to make our own pasta. The whole kitchen is wide open, so you can see what the chefs are up to. Good New Orleans food, good wine, and good service. No tablecloths. Fun. Casual. The longest bar in the French Quarter!"

The dining room was wide, long, and low. As big as any other in town. It looked nothing like the Brennan family's other restaurants. Burning wood in the grill? No tablecloths? No walls between kitchen and dining room? Unheard of. Even empty, it had the look of a lively, social place. "This would be a great spot to do a regular live radio show," I suggested.

"That's a good idea!" said Ella. I told her I knew who the perfect host would be. In the end, she went with the idea, but with a different host.

Mr. B's Bistro proved different, all right. And in more ways than even the forward-thinking Brennans expected. It was busy from its first day. Previously, nobody went to a brand-new restaurant until hearing about it from other people. But word of this place spread virally among restaurant-goers. After a week, you couldn't get into the place without advance planning. The farther that day recedes into the past, the more the opening of Mr. B's looks like the first day of a new epoch in New Orleans cooking and eating. It represented a sharp turn in local dining habits.

And it was a pivotal moment for the Brennans, who loomed very large in the development of the New Orleans restaurant scene and my coverage of it.

The Brennans

In the last half of the twentieth century, the Brennan family was the most innovative, influential, and interesting force in the New Orleans restaurant world. They were major players on the entire American dining scene, too. A schematic diagram of the who, what, and how of New Orleans dining would show a dense network of lines extending from "The Brennans" to hundreds of now-famous chefs, restaurants, and dishes.

Owen E. Brennan was a Bourbon Street nightclub owner in 1946. His Absinthe House was across the street from Arnaud's, the city's leading gourmet restaurant. When "Count" Arnaud Cazenave came in for drinks at Brennan's joint, Owen kidded the Frenchman about the complaints he was always hearing about the food at Arnaud's. Arnaud told Owen that he had no room to talk, because it was well known that no Irishman could possibly understand haute cuisine, let alone operate a decent restaurant. Owen took that as a challenge.

He leased a defunct restaurant space across the street and reopened it as Brennan's French Restaurant. He hired a talented Belgian chef, as well as all the members of his own family who were old enough to work. He then went beyond proving that he could indeed serve food as good as Arnaud's; he made dining out so much more entertaining than the hidebound French-Creole restaurants of the day that Brennan's was soon the talk of the town. He believed that going to a restaurant wasn't just about enjoying good food—it had to leave you laughing. And that began with a personal and friendly greeting. A Brennan (Owen's father, like as not) was always at the door, welcoming the regulars and then distributing blarney all night long in the dining rooms.

All the Brennans seem to have an inborn sense of what constitutes a good party. Some family members became notorious for their ability to continue celebrating when all the other guests were worn down. One of the Brennans' favorite stories is that almost everyone in the family was born in late November or early December—meaning they were conceived around Mardi Gras, the most debauched time of the year in New Orleans. But the Brennans took the concept of unfettered restaurant festivity to new frontiers, managing to expand it into the unlikely breakfast hours, complete with special cocktails and wines. Breakfast at Brennan's, which takes about two hours, and fifty or sixty dollars per person to do right, may be the only meal of its kind in the entire world.

After nine years on Bourbon Street, Brennan's moved to its present location on Royal Street, a much larger, more atmospheric venue, with a classic French Quarter courtyard in the center. That transformed Brennan's from merely a popular spot to one of the world's most profitable restaurants. The hundreds of seats were full three meals a day, seven days a week, with diners paying top dollar at all hours.

Although Owen E. Brennan had died (suddenly, at age forty-five) right before the move to Royal Street, Owen's sisters Ella and Adelaide, his younger brother Dick, and his oldest son Pip took over management. The spectacular success of the new Brennan's inspired Ella and Dick to start thinking big. In the 1960s, they began opening

The Brennan Family

The Brennan family looms so large in the local restaurant trade that a novel could be based on it. The saga begins with six siblings from the Irish Channel. Owen E. Brennan, the oldest, opened Brennan's in 1946. The rest followed him into the business sooner or later. He died in 1955. A rancorous split in 1973 between his sons, brothers, and sisters gave Brennan's to his sons Owen, Jr. ("Pip"), Jimmy, and Ted.

Ella Brennan Martin, the dominant force at Brennan's after Owen died, led her generation's retrenchment at Commander's Palace after the 1973 split. She's retired, but she keeps an eye on Commander's, which is now run by Ella's daughter, Ti, and John's daughter Lally. Ella's son Alex owns Brennan's in Houston. Ella won the 2009 James Beard Lifetime Achievement Award.

Dick Brennan began at Brennan's in his teens and with Ella was managing things when the split happened. He and Ella were the key players at Commander's until retirement. He still shows up at the Palace Café, Dickie Brennan's Steakhouse, and the Bourbon House, all owned by Dick's children, Dickie and Lauren.

Adelaide Brennan was in at the beginning. She was a bon vivant who was famed for her parties. She died in 1983.

John Brennan didn't get into the restaurants until the family split. He sold his wholesale food business and became part of Commander's and Mr. B's. He died in the late eighties. Son Ralph owns Bacco, Red Fish Grill, and Ralph's on the Park in New Orleans, and a restaurant in Anaheim. Daughter Cindy owns Mr. B's. Daughter Lally co-owns Commander's Palace and Café Adelaide.

Dottie Brennan Bridgman joined the restaurants in the 1980s. She's retired but is still involved at Commander's Palace.

or buying other restaurants around New Orleans, then in other cities. In the early 1970s, they were on the verge of starting a national chain of premium steakhouses, along the lines of what Ruth's Chris, Morton's, and Palm would build a decade later. By that time all three of Owen's sons were active in the business; along with Owen's widow, they owned a majority of Brennan's. For the most part, though, they deferred to their Aunt Ella and Uncle Dick in management matters. But the steakhouse plan sounded risky to them. The debates that ensued led to an acrimonious split in the Brennan family in 1973. It has never healed; the two sides of the family still don't speak to one another. Lawsuits between them continue to erupt, more than three decades later.

After the papers defining the schism were signed, Owen's sons and their mother took full ownership of Brennan's. All the other restaurants went to their aunts and uncles. Ella and Dick, with their siblings Adelaide, Dottie, and John Brennan, retreated to new headquarters at Commander's Palace.

The Commander's side of the family faced a big problem. Brennan's on Royal Street was the cash cow, supporting most of the other restaurants. Commander's, a century-old restaurant in an even older Garden District mansion, needed a lot of work. Brennan's in Atlanta and Dallas chugged along, but they were hamstrung by the absence of the culture of eating and joie de vivre that energized New Orleans diners. The Houston restaurant did better, because of cross-pollination between that city and New Orleans on the part of the oil business. The steakhouse concept was stone-cold dead. During the next few years, the elder Brennans closed one restaurant after another, until the only ones remaining were Commander's in New Orleans and Brennan's in Houston.

Ella Brennan was particularly devastated by the split. She told me of a night not long after she got settled at Commander's, when she sat in the stunning courtyard of the restaurant with her brothers. The chef prepared a large selection of the menu for them to inspect. "It was beautiful food!" she said. "But almost nobody was in the restaurant. I sat there and cried!"

THE BIG IDEA

Ella did not cry for long. Tough-minded, confident, and innovative, she quickly resumed forward motion.

Ella Brennan's pronouncements have the ring of incontrovertible truth. Even top food authorities like James Beard, Craig Claiborne, James Villas, and Lucius Beebe—all of whom were her close personal friends—listened and believed. She soon convinced her staff and her customers that Commander's would be one of the great restaurants in America.

Making that a reality was a battle, though. Making fundamental changes in a hundred-year-old restaurant isn't easily done. Then Ella forged what she called "a marriage made in heaven." She hired chef Paul Prudhomme.

Paul Prudhomme arrived in New Orleans in 1975 after growing up on a farm in Cajun country and cooking in the big Cajun town of Opelousas. His first big gig was as chef of a restaurant called La Bon Creole, in a French Quarter hotel. Almost as soon as he arrived, Chef Paul began spreading a new culinary faith. His take on the genuine flavors and ingredients of Louisiana sounded so good that hearing him talk about it made one ravenous.

Although the first thing you noticed about him was his famous girth, he was a handsome man with riveting eyes and a grabber of a smile. His personality was as engaging as his cooking. He appeared more frequently on television and radio shows (including mine) than any other local culinarian; it wasn't long before most people could name Chef Paul—the only local chef they could. Restaurants and other chefs consulted with him to get that kind of energy into their kitchens.

Ella Brennan thought Paul had the answers to a lot of questions. She hired him in 1976 to be executive chef over all her restaurants. Between the two of them, they hatched the Big Idea:

"We threw out the interchangeable French menu every New Orleans restaurant had had for a million years," Ella said. "We replaced it with local everything." That drastically changed the food at Commander's. For example, trout amandine—the restaurant's most popular fish dish—got a makeover. "We don't grow almonds in Louisiana!" Ella said. "Why not do it with pecans from our backyard?" Using not only pecans, but a well-seasoned, Cajun-influenced brown sauce, incomparably more robust and interesting than the old beurre noir, Chef Paul revised the dish. Out went crabmeat Imperial, a polite old standby; in came crabmeat and corn bisque, loaded with cream and Creole seasonings. The new menu was full of such transformations.

The timing was ideal. New Orleans classic restaurant cuisine had become motionless, and newspapers like *Figaro* had instigated a revival of interest in root-level New Orleans institutions, music, and tastes among people of my generation. We baby boomers were beginning to dine in real restaurants; the food Chef Paul was laying down was exactly the sort of thing we could sink our teeth into.

Commander's Palace lifted off, and so did the fortunes of that side of the Brennan family. After having to shrink its empire for six years after the family split in 1973, they reversed the trend in 1979 with the opening of Mr. B's Bistro. It incorporated all of the new ideas Ella and Paul used to retool the menu at Commander's Palace, and then some. Mr. B's nailed the tastes and lifestyles of all the young, self-conscious gourmets.

I was one of those, and I thought Mr. B's was great. Its thick, dark-roux chicken-andouille gumbo was dramatically different from the lighter seafood gumbo served in most restaurants. Within a few years, most gumbos in hip restaurants around town were in the robust, new style. An early Mr. B's dish called shrimp Chippewa evolved into the city's best version of barbecue shrimp—that's easily in the top five or six most delicious of the Creole standards. And the innovative hickory-grilled fish was as enormous a hit as the Brennans had expected. Fish cooked on an open grill was almost unheard of before Mr. B's opened. Within a few years, it was the dominant fish dish on upscale menus all over town.

What really made inroads with customers, though, was that Mr. B's was totally casual. White-tablecloth food without the tablecloth. Jacket-and-tie food for people who preferred jeans. Most first-class restaurants then relied on time-honored recipes, ceremonious service, auspicious surroundings, and, in the worst cases, sheer pretentiousness to persuade customers that the food was good. Mr. B's dispensed with the formalities and put all the emphasis on the food.

It was brilliantly prescient. In my first review of Mr. B's, in *Figaro* in late 1979, I called it the Restaurant of the Eighties. It was the most accurate prediction I ever made. During the next decade, dozens of spots a lot like Mr. B's opened all over town—enough of them to create a whole new restaurant category: gourmet Creole bistros. It quickly became the most popular style of fine dining in New Orleans, and remains so.

THE GOURMET CREOLE BISTROS

The proliferation of the gourmet Creole bistros in the early eighties probably pleased Richard Collin. They satisfied two of his credos: Food is far more important than atmosphere and pretense, and the best flavors are local ones. But Collin gave up writing a restaurant column shortly after Mr. B's opened. For the first of many times, I was the only active restaurant critic in town—and very active at that. By 1980, I was writing not one but two weekly restaurant review columns for different publications. Plus *The New Orleans Menu* monthly magazine. And hosting four hours of radio every day.

The bistros provided much to write about. Their food was not only delicious but innovative. On the other hand, it had a clear Louisiana flavor. It was new enough that it didn't seem like our parents' food, but still familiar enough to ring a bell. The young diners were always ready to try the latest and greatest place, then tell their friends that they'd found the best restaurant in town. When their friends said they'd never heard of it, the praise would grow even louder.

The chefs in the bistros made for good talk, too. They were generally young, well educated, attractive, and willing to have long conversations about their food. That was a big change from the previous generation. With the exception of a few Europeans (most of whom were in hotel restaurants and a few large, freestanding eateries), the typical New Orleans chef at the older spots was someone from a lower-income family who started working in kitchens as a busboy or dishwasher and learned on the job. Many major New Orleans institutions (Galatoire's and Antoine's, to name two) claimed not to have chefs at all, only cooks. I knew of two of these cooks who—despite being firmly in charge of large, famous kitchens—could not read or write. The bistro chefs, by contrast, were often from families at least as well-to-do as those of their customers, and just as well educated.

Jason Clevenger, for instance. He came to prominence in the kitchen at Café Sbisa, then joined his mother JoAnn Clevenger in opening the Upperline, one of the first of the new bistros. He's now a professor of philosophy. Jason's successor at the Upperline, Tom Cowman, was a man of such sophistication that when I ran into him in other grand restaurants, I sometimes didn't recognize him because of the richness of his suits.

These new chefs, borrowing from Commander's and Mr. B's and one another, created a new local menu. Everybody had grilled fish, with an emphatic crust of Creole seasoning. Everybody was incorporating pasta with seafood and Cajun-seasoned cream sauces (before the bistros came along, pasta was the exclusive property of the Italian and Chinese places). Everybody seemed to serve the same newfangled recipe for turtle soup, one easily identified by the presence of spinach. But along with these commonalities, there were plenty of original dishes coming out of the bistros, too.

The first wave of bistros washed across Uptown New Orleans, the neighborhood of the city's most affluent and avid diners. Until then, Uptown had surprisingly few restaurants. The bistros redistributed the patronage, to the detriment of restaurants located far out in the suburbs. Even LeRuth's—widely acclaimed as the best restaurant in the city for twenty years, but inconveniently located on the West Bank—saw its numbers dwindle. Within a few years, it closed. Restaurants in the French Quarter—the center of the restaurant business forever—were deserted by a lot of locals, who found parking for the latest alleged best new restaurant in town a lot easier Uptown. (Mr. B's, in the Quarter, had presciently provided free parking in the garage next door, seemingly in anticipation of this trend.)

These same trends were in motion elsewhere in America, too. But in most other cities, the boomers' growing demand for fancier restaurants was met by the restaurant chains. Starting as hamburger vendors, they moved upscale with their customers, creating the illusion of better dining, while still serving more hamburgers than anything else. Only in New Orleans was a distinctive, encyclopedic local cuisine reinvented, from the ground up, while holding on to the flavors and ingredients that made it unique in the first place. So when

Creole and Cajun fever swept across the country in the mid-1980s, it came as no surprise to New Orleanians.

CHEF PAUL'S BIG SPLASH

Not long after Mr. B's opened in July 1979, I had lunch there with Chef Paul, in the window seat closest to the bar. At the end of the bar stood John Brennan, sipping his cloudy, pale-green Pernod and water. John was the older brother of Ella and Dick Brennan, and his kids Ralph, Cindy, and Lally managed Mr. B's. I remember all those details because of what Chef Paul told me that day. "I leased a little place on Chartres Street," he confided. "Before I go to work at Commander's, I get up real early. I go to the French Market and buy whatever looks great. Then I get lunch started over there. Just some simple Cajun food and some other things I've been thinking about."

I had lunch at K-Paul's Louisiana Kitchen not long after that. I remember eating something called "the po' man's filet," a ground-beef steak with a serious slam of Cajun pepper and flavor; the whole platter, which was filled very amply with good sides, cost four dollars. I also had a Cajun martini, a Ball jar filled with vodka marinated with hot peppers. "It's the only cocktail we have," Chef Paul told me. "It's so big and hot that's it's impossible to drink more than one." Part of the reason for that may have been to discourage the building's former customers; K-Paul's was located in what was previously a bar, whose regulars could not be called upscale. Paul was after a more-culinarily-appreciative crowd.

He got it. Seemingly overnight, K-Paul's (the *K* was for Chef Paul's wife and partner, Kay Hinrichs) had a line running down the block every day at lunchtime. To fit more people in, "community seating" was established—you'd share your table with others. Most people liked that as much as they liked the food. And they were crazy about the food.

Then Chef Paul left the Brennans (who wished him well), opened K-Paul's for dinner, let the prices rise to market levels, and presided over the most-discussed restaurant in New Orleans. Perhaps in America.

K-Paul's had the hottest dish in town, too—in more ways than

The Interchangable Creole Menu

Before about 1978, almost every white-tablecloth restaurant in New Orleans served most and perhaps all of these dishes, with modest variations. Based on the menu at Antoine's in the early 1900s, the menu evolved only very slowly for most of the next century. Most of these dishes are still widely served around New Orleans, but only a handful of the most traditional restaurants still limit their kitchens to this catalogue.

Shrimp Rémoulade

Crabmeat Ravigote

Baked Oysters Rockefeller

Baked Oysters Bienville

Baked Oysters a Third Way
(No two versions were alike, but every restaurant had this, so they could serve "oysters 2-2-2," a half dozen with three kinds of oysters, two of each.)

Seafood Gumbo

Turtle Soup

Vichyssoise

Trout Meunière

Trout Amandine

Trout Pontchartrain
(topped with crabmeat and butter or a small soft-shell crab)

Pompano en Papillote

Poached or Broiled Redfish Hollandaise

Bouillabaisse

Shrimp Creole

Fried Soft-shell Crabs

Chicken Clemenceau
(or Bonne Femme or Pontalba)

Chicken Bordelaise

Tournedos Marchand de Vin

Tournedos Béarnaise

Grilled Lamb Chops with Mint Jelly

Brabant Potatoes

Creamed Spinach

Asparagus Hollandaise

Bread Pudding

Caramel Custard

Crêpes Suzette

Bananas Foster

Chicory or Pure Coffee

As interesting as what items composed the interchangeable menus is what was missing from them. Few of them had crawfish dishes, pork as a central item, duck, or veal. All of those were much enjoyed in homes; some of them were common in neighborhood cafés or Italian restaurants. But it wouldn't be until the advent of the gourmet Creole bistros in the early 1980s that those dishes became common on menus.

one. Blackened redfish was a large, vividly fresh fillet of red drumfish, encrusted with a Cajun blend of seasonings. (Chef Paul would later bottle the stuff and do very well with it.) The fish was dipped in melted butter and slammed into a skillet so hot that flames and billows of smoke leapt up. In an amount of time best measured in seconds, it was dark and crunchy at the skin, but still juicy inside.

Prepared with the skill of Chef Paul, blackened redfish is as exciting a dish as I can imagine. It wasn't long before chefs everywhere tried to cook it—usually without much luck, because they wouldn't take it to the extremes Chef Paul did. What with the smoke and flames, you couldn't really make it at home unless you did it outside. Or had a powerful exhaust system. When Chef Paul made appearances around the country, it wasn't uncommon for the dish to kick off smoke alarms.

K-Paul's continues to serve big-flavor food to this day. But in the long run Chef Paul's next plan made an even more important contribution. He felt it important to inspire a new generation of young chefs. And because he was so charismatic, the profession soon swelled locally with new practitioners. These were the young chefs who, only a few years later, in the 1980s, created the buzz at the gourmet Creole bistros. Many went on to open their own restaurants, which always seemed to have a way of making it to best-of-the-best lists. Frank Brigtsen (Brigtsen's), Greg Sonnier (Gabrielle), and Jack Leonardi (Jacques-Imo's) had the biggest hits. New Orleans kitchens are full of K-Paul's alumni, most of whom probably would never have gone into the business at all—let alone as far as they did—without the influence of Chef Paul.

K-Paul's was a chef's paradise. For a long time, the place was closed on Saturdays and Sundays; having the whole weekend off was unheard of for restaurant workers. Getting the food to the table at its peak took precedence over everything else, including the service standard that everybody should be served their course at the same time. Food came out when it was ready. Relatively little attention was paid to dining room comforts; for many years, K-Paul's remained much the way Chef Paul found it. No tablecloths. Paper napkins. Very inexpensive utensils. On the other hand, nothing was spared in terms of food cost. K-Paul's chefs had the best of everything

The Nouvelle Creole Menu

After the Brennans and Paul Prudhomme abolished the old inter-changeable Creole menu in the late 1970s, they replaced it with a collection of dishes that themselves soon became commonplace in New Orleans restaurants. Most of them still are. The style of cook-ing that those dishes represented has come to be called "nouvelle Creole." Here are some of the greatest hits in that style:

Crab and Corn Bisque

Oyster and Artichoke Soup

Chicken-andouille Gumbo with a Dark, Thick Roux

Shrimp with Andouille Sausage

Seafood Pasta with Tasso and a Rich Cream Sauce

Trout with Pecans

Blackened Redfish

Wood-grilled Fish with Creole Seasoning and Beurre Blanc

Grilled Chicken with Andouille Sausage and Creole Mustard Sauce

Pannéed Veal with Fettuccine Alfredo

Grilled or Smothered Rabbit

Cajun-style Smothered Duck

Steak with Cajun Debris Sauce

Crème Brûlée

Bread Pudding Soufflé

to cook. It was the Mr. B's idea (which Chef Paul had helped to cre-ate in 1979, of course) taken to an extreme.

Some diners, though, were unwilling to abandon the familiar res-taurant creature comforts, no matter how good a chef was. On my radio shows, after a couple of years of hearing only from people who were thrilled by the K-Paul's experience, I started to get callers who were put out by the inconveniences of dining there. Their per-spective was the opposite of a chef's.

Although I never gave K-Paul's lower than a three-star rating (it currently has four), since I write for other diners rather than restaurateurs, these matters had to be noted. Especially after K-Paul's had become rather expensive. Why paper napkins? Why just two wines? Why no reservations? These were not unreasonable questions for a customer to ask. So I asked them.

One spring day, I got a call from Steve Taylor, a friend of Chef Paul's and the writer of a wine column during my tenure at *New Orleans* magazine. He invited me to take a ride on the Goodyear blimp. Chef Paul had planned to go, but he had a schedule conflict and couldn't make it. Steve told me I could fill the open seat. Floating around in a blimp is a unique experience. It's quiet; it moves on waves of air as a boat would; it tilts down during its descent at an angle that takes your breath away. But that's not what I remember most about that day. After the flight, the crew and the other people on board went to K-Paul's for dinner. I had crawfish étouffée. Not surprisingly, it was terrific. Dark roux, lots of fresh crawfish at the peak of the season, seasoning levels at that delicious edge between pleasure and pain. (It's still the best version around.)

During the dinner, Chef Paul was at his usual table in the back of the restaurant, talking with—of all people—David Letterman. I never missed Letterman's show then, and I had to meet him. I threw a few superlatives at Letterman regarding his show, and he reeled back in mock shock. Chef Paul said to me, "After you're finished, I want to tell you something."

What he wanted to tell me was that he didn't want me in his restaurant anymore. I wasn't the first to be banned. Richard Collin was definitely on the you-know-what list. So, for over a decade I didn't dine at K-Paul's. I have since gone back quite a few times—always recognized, but never asked to leave. I don't really know what my status is there now. I also don't know what brought his request on. I've asked lots of people who ought to know, but they don't. Chef Paul and I have had brief, cordial conversations, but I haven't felt comfortable enough to explore the matter.

I suppose it's impossible for a restaurant critic who speaks frankly to avoid becoming persona non grata here and there. This wasn't the only time it happened to me. But I wish it hadn't happened at K-Paul's. I missed eating that étouffée, blackened fish, and filet mignon with debris. And I miss the friendship I had with Chef Paul, who did more than anybody else to let everybody know how good Louisiana food is when it's cooked right.

The Great New Orleans Trout Makeover

In the 1970s, trout amandine was without question the most popular fish dish on white-tablecloth restaurant menus throughout New Orleans. And then came the revolution. Ella Brennan and chef Paul Prudhomme at Commander's Palace remade the dish with a Louisiana flavor—instead of almonds, they used local pecans. The sauce went from a toasty beurre noir to a darker, thicker, much more intense affair. The dish spread quickly to other restaurants. Except for a handful of older restaurants, trout with pecans has replaced trout amandine. The preparation below also works very well with fried soft-shell crabs.

Here are before and after recipes.

Trout Amandine Old Style

1 tsp. salt
¼ tsp. black pepper
1 cup flour
4 fillets speckled trout, about 8 oz. each
2 sticks butter
2 Tbs. lemon juice, strained
1 Tbs. Worcestershire sauce
1 tsp. red wine vinegar
1 cup slivered or sliced almonds

1. With a fork, stir the salt and pepper into the flour. Rinse the fish fillets, and pat them with a paper towel (but don't dry completely). Dredge through the seasoned flour, shaking off the excess.

2. Melt one stick of the butter in a saucepan over medium-high heat. When it begins to bubble, sauté the fish fillets, two at a time, about three minutes on each side, or until golden brown. Allow excess butter to drain back into the pan. Keep the fish warm.

3. Add the other stick of butter to the pan, along with the lemon juice, Worcestershire, and vinegar. Whisk the pan ingredients to blend, and bring to bubbling again.

4. Add the almonds, and lower the heat a little. Cook almonds until they just begin to turn a little brown at the edges. Spoon the sauce and the almonds over trout fillets, and serve immediately.

SERVES FOUR.

AFTER

Trout with Pecans

Pecan Butter

3 Tbs. butter

2 Tbs. roasted pecans

3 Tbs. lemon juice

1½ tsp. Worcestershire sauce

Sauce

2 Tbs. flour

2 Tbs. water

½ cup shrimp or fish stock

½ cup Worcestershire sauce

3 Tbs. lemon juice

2 sticks butter, softened

Fish

3 Tbs. salt-free Creole seasoning

2 Tbs. salt

2 cups flour

2 eggs

½ cup milk

4 trout fillets, each about 8 oz.

1 cup clarified butter

8 oz. roasted pecan halves

1. PECAN BUTTER: Place all pecan butter ingredients into the container of a food processor or blender. Cover and process to a smooth puree. Set aside.

2. SAUCE: In a small bowl, combine flour and water to make a smooth paste. In a small saucepan, bring stock, Worcestershire sauce, and lemon juice to a light boil.

3. Whisk about ⅓ cup of the hot stock mixture into the flour paste. Then gradually pour the flour mixture back into the saucepan, stirring constantly with the whisk, and bring to a boil. Whisk in the softened butter, one tablespoon at a time. Keep sauce warm.

4. FISH: Blend the Creole seasoning and salt into the flour in a wide bowl. Beat the eggs with the milk in a second wide bowl.

5. Dust the trout fillets lightly with the seasoned flour, then pass them through the egg wash, and dredge through the seasoned flour.

6. In a large skillet, heat half of the clarified butter over medium-high heat until a sprinkling of flour sizzles in it. Add three fillets of trout and sauté three or four minutes, until golden brown, turning once. Transfer fillets to serving platter, and keep warm. Add the rest of the butter to the pan and sauté the remaining trout.

7. Spread pecan butter over trout, sprinkle with roasted pecans, top with the sauce, and serve immediately.

SERVES FOUR.

Chef Paul Prudhomme dumps sauce over my head in a staged photo in the courtyard of Commander's Palace in 1978. The photo was on the cover of *Figaro* for an article about what chefs think of restaurant critics. ©1978 Christopher R. Harris.

CHAPTER FOUR

A Mentor Resets the Dials

THE OTHER SIDE OF THE TABLE

In a photograph on the cover of a 1979 issue of *Figaro*, chef Paul Prudhomme appears delighted to dump a pot of gloppy sauce over my head. The staged scene illustrated an article about what chefs thought of restaurant critics. It was pretty funny, except that I was never able to get that gunk out of my jacket. The picture was taken in the courtyard of Commander's, one of the two or three most beautiful and atmospheric places to dine in New Orleans. A few years later, I had another memorable encounter in that courtyard, involving another cover story. I wish I'd worn a jacket that day, too.

I'd just published a review of Commander's as the lead story in *The New Orleans Menu*. I gave the place two stars. Reading it now, I can't figure out why my rating was so low. The restaurant's bad old days were well behind it. It was the interregnum between Chef Paul and Emeril Lagasse (more on Emeril later), but the kitchen was in the throes of developing dishes so good and so popular that many of them are now considered classics.

It was a warm day, and I arrived for lunch in shirt and tie. I started with the corn and crab bisque, replete with jumbo lump crabmeat, fresh corn, and cream. As I ate it, the waiter appeared, with a bottle of Chateau St. Jean Chardonnay. "I didn't order that," I said, as he began uncorking it.

"Mr. Dick told me to bring it to you," the waiter replied.

"I don't take free stuff," I said. Restaurants are always offering, but I found early on that accepting such offers affected my judgment.

"You'll have to explain that to Mr. Dick," he replied, ignoring my protest and pouring the wine anyway.

Although he kept a lower profile than his in-your-face, doctrinaire sister Ella, Dick Brennan was just as strong a force in the management of Commander's Palace (and Brennan's, too, until the family split). Ella described Dick once as "a true Irish Channel character." She knew one when she saw one, too. The Brennans grew up in the Irish Channel, the part of New Orleans along the riverfront between downtown and the Garden District. In the days they lived there, the Channel was still very Irish, largely lower income, and a bit rough.

Dick is a classic tall, dark-haired, fair-skinned, blue-eyed Irishman. A star athlete in his youth, he still looks athletic now that he's in his seventies. He has Ronald Reagan's hairline and Bing Crosby's smile. But his most distinctive quality is his voice. It combines a deep timbre and a mild stutter with the Irish Channel rhythm, vocabulary, and pronunciation (and is not unlike a Brooklyn accent).

Meeting Dick for the first time, some people take him for an unlettered goofball. He is anything but. He is well educated and has seen the world, led organizations, and won his share of awards. He cofounded the Krewe of Bacchus, an organization that in the 1960s renovated the Mardi Gras parade and prevented the celebration from becoming boring (as it was beginning to be). He invented the Sunday jazz brunch—today a fixture around New Orleans and elsewhere. Dick commands the highest regard from other people in the business, especially his former employees. Paul Prudhomme and Emeril Lagasse consider Mr. Dick (as they and everyone else who ever worked for him call him) among the world's most astute restaurateurs.

To relate to his employees, Dick amplifies his Irish Channel persona. He comes across not as the Boss, but as just another guy from the streets. It works. You remember what he tells you.

Anyway, he sure made me hear and remember what he told me that day. I had finished my corn and crab bisque, and I was enjoying redfish Grieg—a large, fresh fillet with a brilliant, buttery sauce of crabmeat and shrimp, all a few hours fresh out of local waters— when I noticed Dick's tall form looming over the table. "Hello, Tom! Mind if I sit down and try some of your wine?"

"It's your wine," I replied. "Have a seat!"

We shortly killed that bottle. Another appeared without my noticing. When you empty a bottle of wine at Commander's, there's another one waiting nearby, ready to refill your glass in seconds, making itself hard to refuse. The chef wanted us to try some lamb chops; Jordan Cabernet arrived. We had dessert; a bottle of Cristal Champagne was popped and poured before I could make a move to stop it. We drank all of that. Then we moved on to Hine Cognac.

The conversation began with Dick's usual good humor. We talked about the weather, sports, food, and restaurants. Then came a disarming poke: "How can you come into a place like this without a jacket?" he asked. Well, my rationale went, it's just lunch, and there is no jacket rule at lunch, is there? Then, another. "You haven't been to France, huh?" And, "Have you ever thought about spending some time working in a restaurant kitchen to see what's going on?"

I began to feel a chill. The armor of respectability that I supposed I had earned working for ten years as a restaurant critic was being dented and knocked off, piece by piece. And then came an exchange remembered vividly by everybody working at Commander's Palace that day. (Don't ever believe that waiters don't know everything going on at every table in the room.) Dick pointed his finger at me, and, speaking pure Irish Channel, with all the long vowels stretched five or six times longer than normal, he said, "Leave me tell you something, Tawm. I'm Irish and you're Irish. And I'm telling you: Yooooooou . . . dooooon't . . . knooooow . . . *nothin'* about food. You don't know the ABCs. You need to get some education. Now look. I'm gonna send you to France. I'll give you $5,000 to go there and learn somethin'. You gotta give it back to me when you can. But if you gonna keep writing about restaurants and foooooood . . . that's what you gotta do."

I didn't know what to say. Whatever it was that made me credible to readers and radio listeners seemed to add up to very little at that moment.

We remained at the table for hours, the excellent alcohol continuing to flow. I can't remember where the conversation went. Dick finally got up and said, "You call me about France, you hear? I mean it. And let's have lunch again. I enjoyed it." He walked with me out of the restaurant and left me on the sidewalk as he turned to continue down the three blocks to his home.

I knew Dick was right. I did not know enough for a person who posed as an expert. The theory behind my work so far—that all a critic needs to know is whether he likes the food or not—now seemed a lame dodge. My biggest deficiency was that I didn't cook. At all. I was still single, and I ate every meal in restaurants—at least two a day, seven days a week. Even during the two years I lived with the woman I almost married, we never ate at home. I could tell you more about the relative merits of the local restaurants than anyone else—but I couldn't go deep into matters of ingredients and techniques. When callers on the radio show asked me for complicated recipe advice, I guessed and danced my way around the subject.

I never called Dick about France, and he never brought it up again. But from that moment on he treated me like a friend and an OK guy. He invited me to his annual St. Patrick's Day lunch, which filled Commander's Patio Room with other Irish Channel characters, all wearing jackets and ties. It inevitably turned into a loud party with jokes, singing, and many empty bottles. I never set foot in Commander's without a jacket again.

Something else came of my association with this new mentor—I began having dinner once a month at Commander's Palace, and just at the time that the future of Creole haute cuisine was emerging. Being there on the front lines, privy to everything happening in the kitchen under an exciting new chef named Emeril was as intense an education about restaurants and cooking as I'd ever have.

Tom, Dick, Marcelle, and Emeril

Marcelle Bienvenu demonstrates a theory I have about New Orleans society. I believe there are only 500 people living in New Orleans. I say that extras are brought in by the hundreds of thousands for Saints games and Mardi Gras, but the rest of the time it's just the 500. Each performs not just one function in your life, but many. You constantly run into the same people, playing different roles.

I first met Marcelle at the University of New Orleans. She booked social programs in the student center. In the course of writing articles for the *Driftwood* about what was going on, I spoke with her often. She was sort of like faculty; I was a student. She was beautiful and clever, and I guess I had a crush on her.

Marcelle turned up again a few years later, at my *New Orleans* magazine Christmas dinner. She was working at Commander's Palace at the time, in various capacities. She had also recently finished writing large sections of the Creole and Acadian volume of Time-Life's *American Cooking* series—a now out-of-print book that many Orleanians treasure in their cookbook collections.

Some months after he chewed me out, Dick Brennan asked if I would join him and Marcelle for lunch. He gave no reason for the particularity of the threesome. Maybe Dick just thought we'd be fun to have lunch with. Or that I could learn something about food from Marcelle.

Marcelle grew up in St. Martinville, a small town in the heart of Cajun country. She speaks with a Cajun lilt. Like most Cajuns, she views cooking and eating lusty food as central to the good life. Also like most Cajuns, she's always laughing and telling jokes about Cajuns and how simple they can be sometimes—especially those that live way out on the bayou with the alligators. (You can tell almost any ethnic joke, even rather heinous ones, as a Cajun joke. All it needs is Cajun dialect and the mention of something like crawfish or boudin in the telling. Cajuns who hear it will laugh loudest and retell it without taking or causing offense.)

So Marcelle, Dick, and I got together for a long, wine-drenched, delicious, and highly amusing lunch in the Garden Room at Commander's. Afterward, Dick thought we needed to do it again. So began a series of monthly repasts that lasted almost ten years. Lunch quickly became dinner, on the first Tuesday of every month, so we could take full advantage of the kitchen's resources.

And we did. The early dinners were cooked by Paul Prudhomme's successor, a talented but comparatively unexciting German chef named Gerhard Brill. But they really began to get interesting when Emeril Lagasse burst out of the future and into Commander's kitchen in 1983. At the time, Commander's Palace was already setting the standard for upscale restaurants in New Orleans. Emeril—still in his twenties during most of his seven years at Commander's—kicked that up a notch, to use his trademark phrase.

Top New Orleans Restaurants, 1984

These are the twenty-four restaurants with the highest ratings in *200 New Orleans Restaurants*, the fourth edition of my restaurant guidebook. By the time this was published, the gourmet Creole bistro era was in full career. The bolded restaurants are still open as of 2010. The entire book from which these ratings came is available to read online: http://www.nomenu.com/200Restaurants1984

★★★★★ **FIVE STARS** ★★★★★
(the maximum rating)

Crozier's
La Provence
LeRuth's
Versailles
Willy Coln's Chalet

★★★★ **FOUR STARS** ★★★★

Antoine's
Arnaud's
*Bozo's
Christian's
Commander's Palace
Del Frisco's
El Patio
Galatoire's
Indulgence
Jonathan
L'Escale
Louis XVI
Maison Andre
Mosca's
Mr. B's
Saffron (Sheraton Hotel)
Sal & Judy's
Savoir-Faire
Trey Yuen

The chemistry was a thrill to observe, especially from the vantage point of our Tuesday dinners. Especially in the first year or two, a white-hot tension between Emeril and the Brennans crackled into the very molecules of the old restaurant and its old-fashioned, genteel dining rooms. Nobody who appreciated new dining experiences would have wanted to miss a second of the transformation that followed. Emeril seethed with new ideas and enthusiasm; the Brennans were paragons of operational and marketing competence. The lookouts of these two forces didn't always mesh—though each appreciated the abilities of the other and went along when the results seemed promising. But they stuck to their guns when they felt strongly about an issue, too.

Nobody relished this game more than Ella Brennan. When she saw she could get more out of somebody by demanding that he do the impossible, she demanded. Emeril was free to build a new engine for this car, but it would have to keep rolling down the road while he fiddled with it. Both Ella and Emeril told me of a critical moment when Emeril lost it with some of his cooks and upset the entire kitchen in the middle of service. Ella grabbed a piece of paper, wrote "You are too damn smart to be so damn stupid!" and shoved it in Emeril's face. She stormed out of the kitchen and left him to sort things out.

The first time I met Emeril, as I recall, was in the middle of one of those maelstroms. Dick Brennan introduced us on one of our "First Tuesday" nights. Emeril was wearing a Rolex, and he gave off a kind of buzzing tension. "He's breaking up with his wife, and he's having a tough time," Dick whispered to me as we went to the table. But something told me there was more to it than that.

The tension between Emeril and the Brennans, far from being destructive, supplied the power for the astonishing evolution in Commander's kitchen during Emeril's seven years there in the late 1980s. It left both the chef and the restaurant working at a height of passion and creativity that neither would have had without the other.

A HUNDRED DINNERS

The First Tuesday dinners I had with Dick and Marcelle stretched across Emeril's entire hegemony at Commander's and into Jamie Shannon's tenure. Both chefs went to the wall for our three-top. They served us the most unusual ingredients cooked in the most adventuresome ways. I remember, for example, the first time fresh foie gras from the Hudson Valley showed up on the menu. It was new to all of us—as it was to most American gourmets then.

Emeril and Jamie (and their rising sous-chefs, who were allowed to stretch by cooking our dinners from time to time) liked having the three of us as guinea pigs. We were eager to try anything they could throw at us. And they had fun with the unlimited budget Dick Brennan allowed for this research and development.

We watched a new form of cuisine unfold from our front-row seats. It wasn't just about reemphasizing local ingredients and cooking traditions, as Chef Paul had done. It was about creating completely novel dishes out of whole cloth, using new and sometimes far-out ingredients, and laying them down in startling but lust-inspiring presentations.

That effort today would engender a great deal of theoretical talk from chefs and critics. Not to mention record-breaking menu prices. And it has in our times brought about a seriousness regarding cooking and eating that I, for one, decry. But at that stage in the evolution of our dinners we were still laughing a lot and acknowledging how great life in New Orleans was, what with food like that.

I wish I had kept a detailed journal of those dinners. It would make a book unto itself. A hundred dinners are hard to recall exactly. We never ate the same dish twice. Except for raw oysters, which all of us loved. And creamed potatoes, which Emeril made so insanely delicious that we had them every month for at least a year. We drank as well as we ate. Dick's taste for grand cru Chablis, Corton Charlemagne, and big, red Burgundies made certain of that. (Ella, an early champion of California wines, gave him some flack about all that French wine.) Even without notes, though, it's easy to remember plenty of high points:

- PRESSED DUCK. Dick felt it was important for Commander's Palace to own a polished-silver duck press, like the ones at la Tour d'Argent in Paris. He also knew it would hardly ever be used in normal service. A duck press crunches the bones and extraneous meat from a duck carcass, releasing blood and other juices for use in making a sauce. The process requires freshly killed wild ducks—not something a restaurant can legally sell. When

Emeril or Jamie went hunting and brought back some ducks, they pressed them for us. They cooked them using recipes ranging from classic Rouennaise style to nouvelle Cajun. It hardly seemed to matter. Not many dishes could beat those pressed ducks. And nothing ever went better with the big Bordeaux wines Dick called for from the cellar.

- FROG MAN. Emeril developed a network of farmers who raised all kinds of specialty foods expressly for Commander's. He'd come out and tell us that his frog man had been by that day, and we'd have a pile of frog legs. He also had a rabbit man, a quail man, a turkey man, a soft-shell crab man, and a long list of men who raised lettuces, tomatoes, herbs, and other vegetables. One month, our First Tuesday dinner did not include a single item from a generic food wholesaler; everything was from local farmers. That was our first look at the most important innovation Emeril brought to Commander's and, later, to his own restaurant. He placed more emphasis on obtaining interesting ingredients than he did on how he cooked them.

- KNIFE-AND-FORK OYSTERS. For one dinner, Emeril found "reef oysters." They were the same *Crassostrea virginica* oysters we eat by the zillions around New Orleans and up the Atlantic Coast, but these came from oil rigs way out in the Gulf of Mexico. Oil rigs, strangely, teem with fish and shellfish. These oysters had attached themselves to the rigs and grown, unmolested, for so long that they were the size of an adult person's hand. We ate them raw, but we needed knives and forks to do it. They tasted even better than oysters of normal size. Then, when Louisiana caviar appeared on our table and surprised us with its excellence, we ate the oysters topped with those fine gray BBs.

- CRAWLING ESCARGOTS. Jamie Shannon once cooked for us the first live snails any of us had ever eaten. To prove their vivacity, Jamie brought out a dinner plate on which a couple dozen snails (the kind that grow and are canned in France) oozed around, some defying gravity on the underside of the plate. You can't herd snails, apparently. Jamie had a brush with the authorities when it came out that it's against Louisiana state law to introduce live snails of that genus into the state. He had to kill them all. I wish I had been around *that* day.

- THE ULTIMATE MENU. Ella Brennan joined us for dinner one First Tuesday night during the Jamie Shannon years. "Tell me a good joke," she ordered Marcelle. "I need one. It's okay if it's dirty." Marcelle obliged with a long tale (most Cajun jokes are) about three backwoods Cajuns gone fishing. Nearing the punchline, one of the Cajuns comes to the dock with a pirogue full of pussy willows (I think I can stop right there). Ella and the rest of us roared.

  When we stopped laughing, Ella picked up the menu and looked it over for about a minute. Then she hit the big card with her hand. "*This* is the best menu in America tonight," she said, leaving no room for dispute.

  I don't recall a single dish on that menu, but I do remember that everything was as innovative as it was irresistible. Those two effects don't often occur together. Only the knowledge that one couldn't eat it all made any of the offerings less alluring, and then, only by a little. It was like being in a brand-new restaurant—but Commander's had opened in 1880!

- TURNING STEAK INTO FISH. On the other hand, one of our most memorable dinners had the least creative menu of them all. Chef Jamie was out of the restaurant that night, and Dick suggested that we have the house steak: a thick, prime, dry-aged sirloin strip. No sauce, just a steak. It was spectacular. Crusty on the outside, juicy in the middle, well seasoned, richly beefy, tender but with a certain satisfying chewiness. Nobody at the table could remember having had better.

  I needed to know how it was cooked; Dick didn't have to call for the chef. "We put it in a smoking black iron skillet, with Creole seasoning and clarified butter. That's how we were going to cook steaks for the Inner Circle Steakhouse" (the proposed name for the dead-in-the-water chain that broke the Brennan family up).

"It sounds like exactly how you blacken redfish," I said.

"That's because somebody said, 'let's do steak like we do fish,'" Dick explained. He said it wasn't Chef Paul's idea (although Paul did come up with the name), but Gerhard Brill's. I remembered that Gerhard used to like making flames leap.

• SAZERAC. We always met for a drink in the bar before our dinners. (As if we needed it.) One hot July evening, Marcelle arrived and told the bartender, "I need something to cool me off. Give me a Sazerac." Six months later, with a frigid wind whistling through the courtyard outside, she said, "Brrr! I need something to warm me up. Give me a Sazerac." A cocktail for all seasons!

Nothing in my career has given me more to write and think about than those hundred dinners. The chefs always had long stories to tell about the food they served us, the topics ranging from where they found the raw materials to the fine points of preparing them; we usually adjourned to the kitchen to watch. If one of us asked the chefs to try an idea we had, they would.

Adding to the entertainment was Dick Brennan and his viewpoint on things. From forty years of patrolling his restaurants—much of that time in the French Quarter—he had a million stories. Dick had dined in all the great restaurants of America and Europe. He knew every interesting restaurateur in the country, many of whom were his personal friends. Dick's perspective on things often seems to emerge from a part of the brain that most people don't possess. Yet it always makes sense. I've thought of writing a little book of things I've heard him say, but the full effect is lost without the Irish Channel delivery. Example: A waiter opened a bottle of wine for us and poured an absurdly small amount into the glass for Dick to taste. Dick pointed at the glass and told the waiter, "Look, put a little more wine in there, 'caaaauuuuse if it's bad, we're gonna throw the whole bottle away." (It's funnier to hear him say it.)

Our First Tuesday dinners ended when Dick had a heart attack. Cardiac problems are a plague on the Brennans; all of Dick's siblings had bypass surgery, except Owen, who died of a heart attack before he could be helped. Dick's son Dickie, who operates three

French Quarter restaurants, had a bypass in his thirties. After our dinner run was over, though, Dick, Marcelle, and I would occasionally reconvene for a lunch or a dinner; most of the time we'd spend it reminiscing about those amazing First Tuesdays.

Marcelle, as one of the 500 People, continues to show up in the same places I do. She's a busy writer, with a rightly popular newspaper column about Cajun and Creole cooking in *The Times-Picayune*. She wrote a book of reminiscences and recipes, called *Who's Your Mama, Are You Catholic, and Can You Make a Roux?* It is as delightful as its title. She also cowrote several of Emeril's cookbooks, including the one I think of as his best: *Louisiana Real and Rustic.*

I was in my early thirties when my friendship with Dick began. He was about the age I am now—late fifties. He was the mentor I needed at the time. My father, who passed away not long after Dick confronted me in Commander's courtyard, did not comprehend what I did for a living, pleased though he was by my success at it; Dick knew everything about that world. He even talked a lot like my dad. I always look forward to hanging out with him. He's by quite a large margin the most interesting person I've come to know on my beat.

Veal Marcelle

This dish was created by chef Gerhard Brill at Commander's Palace in honor of Marcelle Bienvenu. Marcelle worked at Commander's for a few years; opened her own restaurant outside Lafayette, Louisiana; cowrote most of Emeril's cookbooks; and is the author of the best food column in the New Orleans newspaper *The Times-Picayune*. She, Dick Brennan, and I had dinner together at Commander's monthly for almost ten years. This is a really rich dish—a Creole variation of veal Oscar. The recipe is adapted from one in *The Commander's Palace Cookbook* (1984), by Ella and Dick Brennan.

8 slices veal, about 3 oz. each
Creole seasoning
All-purpose flour
3 Tbs. butter
½ cup green onions, thinly sliced
2 medium shallots, chopped
1 cup jumbo lump crabmeat
2 tsp. Worcestershire sauce
1 cup hollandaise (see page 72)

1. Pound the veal between two sheets of plastic wrap. Season with Creole seasoning, and coat very lightly with flour.

2. Heat the butter in a skillet until it bubbles. Add the veal and cook until golden brown on both sides, turning once. This happens quickly; don't overcook.

3. Remove the veal, and keep it warm. Add the green onions, shallots, crabmeat, and Worcestershire to the pan. Stir while cooking, for about a minute.

4. Place two slices of veal on each plate, and divide the pan contents among plates. Top with hollandaise, and serve immediately.

SERVES FOUR.

Hollandaise

Hollandaise is one of the "mother sauces" of classical French cooking, and it is widely used around New Orleans, where it usually contains an extra pinch of cayenne. It's not hard to make if you can keep it from breaking, which will happen if the sauce gets too hot once the butter goes in. I avoid this by whisking in the butter in a softened, not melted, form.

Hollandaise should be made right before it's needed. If you try to keep it warm, it might break. If that happens, you can sometimes bring it back by adding a little warm water. If that doesn't work, drop a single egg yolk into a fresh bowl, and slowly whisk the broken sauce into it.

2 egg yolks
1 Tbs. red wine vinegar
1 Tbs. warm water
1 stick plus 3 Tbs. butter, softened
Pinch cayenne
1 tsp. lemon juice

1. Whisk the egg yolks and the vinegar briskly in a metal bowl set over a saucepan with about an inch of simmering water at the bottom. If you see even a hint of curdling in the eggs, take the bowl off the heat, but keep whisking. Keep going back and forth, on and off the heat, until the mixture turns thick and lightens in color. Whisk in a tablespoon of warm water.

2. Begin adding the softened butter, a pat at a time. After about a fourth of the butter has been added, you'll begin to see a change in the texture of the sauce. At that point, you can step up the addition of the butter a bit. Keep going till all the butter is incorporated.

3. Whisk in the cayenne and the lemon juice, and serve immediately.

MAKES ABOUT ¾ CUP.

Sazerac Cocktail

The Sazerac has a strong claim to having been the original cocktail. It was created by Antoine Peychaud, who, like many other makers of cocktails in the early 1800s, was a pharmacist. His version used Sazerac-du-Forge Cognac, absinthe, and the bitters Peychaud created in his own shop. Over the years it evolved into a rye whiskey–based drink, with an absinthe substitute like Pernod or Herbsaint. Peychaud's Bitters remained essential. In 2008, the state legislature in Louisiana declared the Sazerac the official cocktail of New Orleans. In its classic form, it's an inch of strained, high-proof liquor in the bottom of a chilled glass, with a lemon twist. It's an acquired taste, but a good one.

Splash of Pernod, Herbsaint, or Ricard
1 generous shot-glassful of rye whiskey
1 Tbs. simple syrup
4 to 5 dashes Peychaud's Bitters
1 slice lemon peel

1. Splash the Pernod or other liqueur into a chilled old-fashioned. Twist the glass around to coat the sides, and pour out the excess contents, allowing only the coating to remain. (The pros throw the glass up in the air with a spin, and let the excess Pernod disperse by centrifugal force).

2. Combine the other liquid ingredients in a second glass, filled with ice. Stir vigorously to blend well. Strain into the liquor-coated class. Twist the lemon peel over the glass, and drop it in.

MAKES ONE SAZERAC.

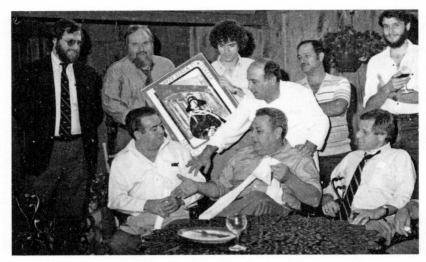

The old guard of New Orleans chefs gather for lunch at La Provence in 1984. From left, seated: Chef Goffredo Fraccaro of La Riviera, Warren Leruth of LeRuth's, wine merchant Richard Jacoves. Standing: the author, Channel Four news director Phil Johnson, writer Frank Levy, Chef Chris Kerageorgiou of La Provence, Chef Sal Impastato of Sal and Judy's, and an unidentified guest.

CHAPTER FIVE

All Food, All the Time

A BREAK AND A BOOM

During the time spanned by my enrichment program with Dick, Marcelle, and Emeril, it became clear that it was time for me to shift all my career eggs into one basket. It was a conscious, considered plan, but outside forces pushed in that direction, too. My daily talk show came to an end in 1983, when the station changed formats from talk to rock. After *Figaro* went bust during my editorship of it, I decided to give up on a generalized career in the media and specialize in covering food and wine exclusively.

I thought this had a good chance of working, even though freelancing can keep one awake at night worrying about where the next check is coming from. But the timing couldn't have been better. A restaurant boom was under way. The gourmet Creole bistros were sprouting across the city. Many new major hotels and restaurants were opening, to take advantage of the tourism expected from the 1984 New Orleans World's Fair.

And there was one other new attraction: world cuisines. New Orleans, like many other places with a strong regional cooking style, has always been suspicious of ethnic cooking. We had a few Chinese and Mexican places (most of them mediocre), and that was about it. French and Italian hardly counted as ethnic, since most of those had been around long enough to hybridize with Creole cooking. But restaurants were the new rock and roll for a lot of boomers. They dined out much more frequently than their parents did and were far more likely to try new food. When a critical mass of diners appeared, many would-be ethnic restaurateurs were waiting for the chance.

In about five years, the number of noteworthy eateries in New Orleans doubled. I know this because I was publishing my restaurant guide every year or two. In 1981, it was possible to cover the essence of the dining scene in a hundred reviews without leaving out any important establishments. By 1986, this could not be done with fewer than two hundred.

Even with their increased numbers, the restaurants were busier than they had been when just half their number were around. The New Orleans food culture was spreading to parts of the population that had previously ignored restaurants above the sandwich-shop level. Meanwhile, we continued to love our red beans, gumbo, poor boys, and fried seafood. In fact, eating in restaurants was such a strong interest among New Orleanians that another radio station hired me to give daily reviews shortly after I lost the previous gig. With the exception of the two months following Katrina, I haven't been off the air since.

INTO THE KITCHEN

My loose schedule gave me the chance to build my skills as a cook. In doing so, I discovered a principle I've preached to my listeners and readers ever since: Really, basic cooking is not difficult. What most people lack—the lack of which scares them away from cooking—is the knowledge of what tastes good. Having a clear idea of how a finished dish should look, smell, and taste does more for one's cooking than any technique or ingredient. I already knew what I wanted to taste in a large number of dishes; I'd learned that from the hundreds of restaurant reviews I'd written.

The first ambitious dish I undertook to re-create in my kitchen was oysters Rockefeller, in the style of Antoine's, the originator of the dish. The recipe is such a secret that Roy Guste, Jr., didn't include it when he wrote the otherwise comprehensive *Antoine's Restaurant Cookbook*. And he's the great-great-grandson of Antoine Alciatore! However, I knew exactly what Antoine's oysters Rockefeller tasted like. I was determined to puzzle out how those flavors were arrived at.

The sleuthing was fun. I knew the recipe contained no spinach, but what *were* those greens? A cook at Antoine's gave me a hint:

Most of the ingredients for the sauce appeared in the restaurant's peculiar, cubist Bayard salad. So, chopped celery, parsley, green onions, and anchovies. In the finished dish, it was easy to detect a blond roux and bread crumbs. Another cook, at Brennan's, told me he thought there was a touch of tomato in there—maybe even ketchup. Where did the anise flavor come from? It occurred to me that Peychaud's Bitters—an essential ingredient in a Sazerac cocktail, originally made in a pharmacy around the corner from Antoine's—might provide that.

I tried all these ideas, tweaking the recipe as I got closer to the flavor and texture of the original. I wound up throwing out the Peychaud's. When I replaced some of the celery with fennel, the recipe took a big leap forward. The anchovies were a good addition, too. I quit after the fiftieth effort. It tasted right to me by then, even though the color was more brown than green. (I later learned this was because Antoine's used green food coloring in its sauce.)

Considering the complexity and secrecy of the recipe, it really wasn't so hard. If that's all there is to cooking, I thought, then I can cook. So, using the same techniques, I worked up the recipes for a bunch of other dishes I liked—most of them from restaurants, a few from family. It became my first cookbook, a minimal tome called *The Ten Best New Orleans Recipes, and a Hundred More*. It was as much a lavish description of those top restaurant dishes as it was a cookbook. A lot of people bought it as a dining guide. Once again, I found that more people like to eat than like to cook.

Next, someone at the radio station saw the booklet and asked me to begin a new daily recipe program. As suddenly as I became a restaurant critic—and with no more formal training—I was now a recipe developer. A few months later, the ABC television station in town recruited me to cover both eating and cooking in a single weekly piece for the local TV news. I'd go to a restaurant with a cameraperson; we'd shoot around the place while I gave a fast review of the food; then we'd head to the kitchen, where the chef would demonstrate a dish. When I took what I knew of the dish home, I then fooled around with it until it tasted right and wrote it down; oftentimes this was the first time the recipe had been put down on paper in language a nonprofessional cook could use. We mailed out the recipes to anyone who asked, and I also ran them in *The New Orleans Menu*.

Producing that show gave me a lot of kitchen practice. It also revealed to me what people liked to cook and eat. The most-requested recipes were familiar local dishes—the kind I would have guessed everyone already knew. Now and then, a clever new dish from a gourmet Creole bistro would grab the viewers. But far more popular were gumbo, barbecue shrimp, crawfish étouffée, and other Creole standards. So maybe all this new cuisine from Emeril and the bistro chefs wasn't penetrating as deeply into the local cooking culture as we all had assumed.

In 1985, chef Andrea Apuzzo and his cousins Roberto and Costantino De Angelis—scions of a family that operates hotels and restaurants in Capri—had opened the most ambitious Italian restaurant New Orleans had ever seen. Unlike its competitors, most of which served what could only be called Creole Italian food, Andrea's emphasized Northern Italian cookery. One day as I was lunching at the restaurant, I asked Chef Andrea for the recipe for veal Tanet, one of his signature dishes. "Let's just go back into the kitchen and I'll show you," he said. I watched and got it all down. We brought the finished dish back to the table and ate it. Andrea—never one to pass up an opportunity to expand his coverage—asked if I'd be interested in helping him write a cookbook.

For more than a year, Chef Andrea and I spent two or three mornings a week in his kitchen, preparing more than 300 dishes. I propped the original laptop computer (yes, a Radio Shack Model 100) on the stove and wrote the recipes as he cooked them. We measured everything carefully—something he'd never done before for most of his recipes. When he did something that mystified me, I asked him why. Sometimes it was just a tic. But in most cases he held forth on why certain procedures were important to a dish.

I learned more about the fine points of cooking from that year of recipe testing than the sum of what I already knew. Andrea's food was very different from the Creole food I was accustomed to cooking and eating. He didn't use roux in anything, for example. He disdained deep-frying. He used much less salt and pepper than was common in New Orleans dishes. Still, I found that much of what

I picked up from Andrea could be applied to Creole and various other styles of cooking. It added a new dimension to my abilities at the stove. I discovered more than a few tools I'd never used before, too. Even so, my earlier principle remained solid. Since I knew what Andrea's food tasted like before I started cooking it, I avoided many mistakes.

La Cucina di Andrea's was a fine cookbook, full of color photos

The Restaurant Critic's Diet

I really did lose sixty pounds by following this plan and doing little else.

Eat all meals in restaurants. Have no food at home at all.

As a restaurant critic would, dine in different restaurants and eat different dishes every day. The more variety, the better.

Order a normal meal for the restaurant and your appetite.

Eat only half of each course. If the food is so delicious that you think you might have trouble stopping halfway, divide the plate in half, and cover one half with a tremendous amount of salt, Tabasco, or both.

Note: Don't ask the waiter to bring you a half portion. Restaurants will not actually do this, but will instead send a smaller but still close to normal amount of food, even when they charge half the price (which they may not). Don't concern yourself with the issue of waste. The food is lost whether you eat it or not. Of course, do not have it packed to take home, unless you really are giving it to the dog.

Don't eat the bread unless it's really unusual or wonderful.

Dessert is okay, but just half.

No serious restaurant critic likes buffets.
Stay away from them completely.

WHAT'S CREOLE? WHAT'S ROUX?

If one would cook Creole and Cajun, this knowledge is essential. Even though no two people agree completely about the details.

One of the great paradoxes of New Orleans cooking is that while it's easy to recognize by taste, it's almost impossible to define. We see this most maddeningly in gumbo. If a hundred New Orleans cooks (native or naturalized) were asked to make gumbo, the result would be a hundred different soups, all of which would be recognizable as gumbo. But it's also possible that someone using all the standard ingredients and techniques for gumbo can wind up with something nongumbo that tastes as if it had come from Ponca City, Oklahoma. I am not the first to draw a parallel between this effect and Louis Armstrong's famous answer when asked to define jazz: "If you have to ask, you'll never know."

But we do know that roux is the cornerstone of a very large number of Creole and Cajun dishes. Not all of them, mind you. But if you can't make a roux, you won't get far as a Louisiana cook. Roux is nothing more than flour mixed with oil (or butter or some other fat) and browned. The practice comes straight out of orthodox French cooking. French chefs for the most part have left roux behind—although knowing how to make it is still considered an essential skill. But roux lives on in Louisiana, where the making of it has quasi-religious aspects. There are two universal precepts for making a roux:

1. Never stop stirring the roux while cooking it. Otherwise it will burn, and then you have to throw it away and start over.

2. While stirring, never let roux splash onto your hand or arm. Hot roux burns all the way to the bone (or feels that way). This is why most roux is made in a saucepan instead of a skillet.

Then there's this commandment, for which there are dispensations:

3. Have the onions, celery, and bell peppers (aka "the Holy Trinity") all chopped up and ready to go into the roux once it's reached the right color. The vegetables will caramelize in the lavalike roux and cool it down at the same time.

The Louisiana style of making roux is to brown the flour in the fat itself. (In France, the flour is usually browned on its own, in a dry pan on the stove or in the oven.) How brown you let the roux become depends on the recipe. A blond roux is a pale tan. The darkest roux is such a dark brown that it's almost black. Somewhere in between is what Creole cooks call a red roux—one the color of a no-longer-shiny penny. The best tool for stirring is a "roux stick"—a wooden spoon with a flat outer edge.

Every Creole and Cajun cook has his or her own roux rituals and will say that these are critically important. Here are mine. (See list below.)

To those who don't make it, the whole idea of roux sounds less than appetizing and like a lot of work. Why add more fat and carbohydrates to extend, color, or thicken a soup or a sauce? Well . . . if you have to ask, you'll never know.

Tom's Roux Rules

Tom's Roux Rule 1

Start making the roux over high heat, and slowly lower the heat as you go. The darker a roux gets, the faster it gets darker still, because of its own accumulated internal heat. It's much easier to control the process if this is counteracted by adding less heat to the pan.

Tom's Roux Rule 2

Stir in a cup or so of the stock or other liquid from the recipe to cool the roux and vegetable mixture enough that it stops cooking. After that, add the roux to the stock, instead of the stock to the roux. (The latter is what my mother and most other home cooks do.) That way you can control the amount of roux in the dish to a fine point.

Tom's Roux Rule 3

The standard roux recipe begins with equal amounts of oil and flour. I find that a three-to-four oil-to-flour ratio works better. (This is a matter of controversy among cooks.)

and great recipes, if I do say so myself. Twenty years later, it doesn't seem dated. It's still one of the books I refer to most often, and I only hear good things from people who buy it.

After writing *La Cucina di Andrea's*, my own recipe work seemed vastly easier. And my newfound facility at the stove made the radio show I would soon begin much better than the all-eating, no-cooking show I did before.

A New Game, a Broken Recipe

My freelance gamble was a winner. The flexibility it gave me allowed me to take on projects like Andrea's cookbook and to travel much more widely—first to the major food and wine cities of America, then to Europe. I loved what I was doing and believed I was getting very good at it.

My home life was nothing to write home about, however. When you have lunch and dinner in restaurants seven days a week, home becomes a bedroom and a bathroom. That didn't bother me, but it did seem to matter to the women I dated. We were all in our thirties now, and they were becoming more frank about permanent nesting. I felt no such urgency.

My wife says that were it not for her, I would still live that way. I shoot the same charge back at her: She was in her thirties when we met, and she was still living with her parents. But we did meet, and the meeting changed our lives. She hired me for a new daily radio show. Seven months later we were married. It happened as quickly as I'm making it sound.

Mary Ann Connell managed the programming at WSMB, an old AM talk station, whose new owner wanted to clean house and start fresh. (That owner was Marc Winston, yet another diner at our *New Orleans* magazine Christmas dinner in 1975. One of my 500 People!) Mary Ann only knew me a little, and the impression I had made on her was not good. But a friend she trusted urged her to contact me anyway about hosting a food talk show.

I had to think long and hard about her request. On the one hand, it would mean strapping myself to a fixed daily schedule for the first time in years. On the other, my urge to be on the air remained undiminished. Plus, the money they offered me was very serious. I decided to give it a shot. I could always quit, right?

That was July 1988. I still hold that job. But something even bigger came of it. Watching Mary Ann walk around the station pushed my romance button. Unfortunately, she felt no similar warmth at the time. That didn't stop me from tricking her into going out with me. (That's the way she describes it.) We had a pair of comical dates, during which she refused to admit that we were even on a date.

As the second nondate played out, though, we both knew that marriage was inevitable. I had never been in love like that before. And to a woman who thought that gourmet food was just so much hydrogen sulfide waiting to happen! Give her the simple stuff, she said (and still says).

When Mary Ann was fired from the radio station after a few more weeks, we kept our mutual gig going. We were married in February 1989. As soon as possible thereafter we were parents of a son, Jude. Three years later came a girl, Mary Leigh. Mary Ann was a natural mother, and she happily forgot about her career so she could enjoy the experience to the fullest. She mothered brilliantly, and we have two great kids to prove it.

For my part, nothing could surpass the pleasure I got from being a dad. My son gave me a second boyhood, one I relished, as he enjoyed his first. I felt the same kind of joy gazing at my daughter's cute little face at birth, or at the beautiful young woman she'd become during one of the daddy-daughter dinner dates we started having early on.

Jude made his first visit to a restaurant when he was just three weeks old, when Mary Ann and I had a romantic dinner at Brennan's. Baby Jude slept through the meal in a little carrier on the table, next to a basket holding the 1967 Chateau Cos d'Estournel. (Few such dinners went that well.) Until they were preteens, our children were always with us. Mary Ann didn't like leaving the kids with sitters—not even her numerous siblings. On the few occasions when we did, she couldn't keep her mind off what might be happening, and couldn't enjoy the evening.

She did want to be included in dinners at really fabulous places, especially those with the cachet of celebrity. The preopening dinner at Emeril's, for example. It was filled with Emeril Lagasse's many friends in the restaurant business. He wasn't yet famous, but his seven years at Commander's Palace made him the most important chef in New Orleans. It was quite a party.

Among the attendees at Emeril's premiere was Jude, now nine months old. He sat in his high chair among the top princes and patrons of the New Orleans restaurant world, as they partied, drank, and feasted. It was utterly absurd. When I recall the moment, I smile and shake my head at the same time, with fond memory and embarrassment eclipsing the real significance of that opening. It wasn't the first or last time my attempt to be a restaurant critic and daddy at the same time ended up with my not being either one very well.

But what could be done? I didn't want to—and couldn't—give up either role. So we just tolerated the inevitable and frequent contretemps. I'd stay out eating at Commander's Palace with Dick and Marcelle until midnight, then wake up at six o'clock the next morning to drive the kids to school. I'd test-cook my original gourmet dishes during the week, then grill hot dogs over a wood fire in the middle of nowhere for Jude and the other Boy Scouts on weekends. I decried the depredations of chain restaurants on the local food culture, but took the kids to Shoney's, with its offensive but highly kid-friendly breakfast buffet, every Saturday. I had to be unambiguously either critic or daddy at any given moment—and being daddy required willing suspension of taste. It could get a little schizoid at times.

It was the right thing to do, though. As wonderful a life as my pursuit of the culinary heights has given me, nothing could compare with the fifteen years of Saturday morning breakfasts my children and I shared. It was an anchor of our lives, until puberty dislodged it, first for Jude, then Mary Leigh. But those breakfasts left a golden glow in my heart that will last until the day I die (which will probably be from eating all that bacon and all those trans fat–loaded biscuits).

The Eat Club

If I'm remembered for anything after I'm gone, I hope it will be for the New Orleans Eat Club. Launched in the early 1990s, the Eat Club is a series of weekly wine dinners I host in restaurants around town. They're attended by my radio listeners and readers—anybody who wants to come.

My original motivation for the Eat Club was to enhance my coverage of the restaurant scene by borrowing the appetites, time, and money of other diners. All of those resources were in shorter supply after I became a family man with a growing waistline. Meanwhile, the number of restaurants was increasing, and so were changes to the menus in the existing ones. Through the Eat Club, I could sample a wider range of dishes and wines in a single meal than I could have otherwise, with less stress on my no-expense-account budget.

My wife thought the idea of dining out with radio listeners was crazy. During her years as a talk show host, she had a few stalkers emerge from her audience. It's a common experience among radio people; the plot of the movie *Play Misty for Me* is not exaggerated. But I have always enjoyed an audience of unusual quality; selecting for gourmets and cooks selects against weirdos. I go months between crank calls on the air; hosts of other types of programs typically get them hourly.

Eight very pleasant people showed up for the first dinner, hosted by chef Horst Pfeifer at Bella Luna, his stunning eatery in the French Market. The restaurant had great food and a magnificent view of the Mississippi River. (Sadly, it was ruined by Hurricane Katrina and never reopened.) We had five courses, beginning with house-made fettuccine, garnished at the table with grated white truffles. From there, the diners ordered from the menu, each getting something different. I brought eight bottles of wine. We stole this dinner at forty dollars, all-inclusive.

At this table of complete strangers (to one another as well as to me), the conversation came as easily as if we were all family. We talked strictly about food. This food we were eating, the food we loved the last time we were there, the food we loved the last time we were somewhere else, the food we might discover tomorrow. Then how lucky we were to live in a place with such superb, eminently local eats. How naturally the enjoyment came, and how the passion united us!

We even talked about the way we talk about food all the time. I told a story about a radio ad executive who came to town from the

Northeast. Right before he left in frustration a year later, he revealed to me that he couldn't get conversations going when he took clients out to lunch. "I try to talk business, sports, politics, real estate, and—nothing!" he said, shaking his head. "The only thing on their minds is food!" The Eat Club table found that hilarious.

After a few more iterations, the dinners began to grow uncontrollably. When they sold out, listeners got mad at me for not accepting a few more diners. They wanted to sign up for future meals before they were even planned. Chefs loved doing the dinners, even though they generally lost money on them, because of all the on-air talk that came out of them.

I tried to keep a lid on the demand by adding a surcharge, which I turned over to the Second Harvest Food Bank. That only increased the demand. Before the year was out, we were selling out dinners to thirty or forty people every week. The whole-menu format had to be shifted to a set-menu one. And instead of spending the evening at one table, I moved around from table to table, having a course at each one.

We still sell out Eat Club dinners every week. The record for attendance was set at an oyster and lobster dinner at Drago's, the city's leading casual seafood house: 258 people. Drago's had gas grills for the oysters and washtubs for boiling lobsters in the parking lot. I was so busy visiting tables that I didn't get a chance to eat.

Our smallest dinner (after the first few trial runs) hosted sixteen people at a single oval table of sleek polished wood, in the wine cellar of the Windsor Court Grill Room. The chef dictated that number, because he wanted to serve a complex dinner with rare wines. It was scheduled for September 13, 2001. Although restaurants all over America were empty that night, all sixteen Eat Clubbers showed up. It was one evening when we did not talk mostly about food (even though what we were being served was extraordinary).

I recall that the sea scallops were the size of filets mignon and outstanding. Even that night, with the recent news riveting our attention, we didn't forget completely about the comforting pleasures of food. We never do here in New Orleans. In a way, that night was a precursor of how we'd handle another tragedy four years later.

My Oysters Rockefeller

The most surprising request for a recipe I ever received came from Bernard Guste, the fifth-generation proprietor of Antoine's. He wanted to use my recipe for oysters Rockefeller. Antoine's invented the dish in 1899 and has kept the recipe a secret ever since. But they needed something to give the many people who ask for it. Guste told me that my recipe is "embarrassingly close" to the real thing. I'm flattered. And if I do say so myself, he's right. It took me about fifty tries to create a match for the flavor of Antoine's great specialty.

Which does not and never did include either spinach or Mornay sauce, as most recipes call for. Oysters Rockefeller has always been among my favorite Creole-French dishes and one that creates its own special occasion when you make it.

2 cups celery, chopped
1½ cups green onion tops, chopped
2 cups parsley, chopped with stems removed
1 cup fresh fennel, chopped
1 cup watercress, chopped
½ tsp. fresh garlic, chopped
3 anchovy fillets
Liquer from four dozen oysters plus enough water to make two cups
1 tsp. sugar
¼ cup ketchup
1 tsp. salt
1 tsp. white pepper
½ tsp. cayenne
1 Tbs. Worcestershire sauce
2 dashes Peychaud's Bitters
2 drops green food coloring (optional, but authentic)
2 sticks butter
1 cup flour
1½ cups very fine fresh bread crumbs
Four dozen oysters

Preheat oven to 450 degrees.

1. Combine the vegetables and the anchovies in small batches, and chop to a near-puree in a food processor, using just enough of the oyster water to help things along.

2. Combine this green slurry and the rest of the water in a sauce-pan, and cook over low heat, stirring every now and then, until the excess water is gone but the greens remain very moist. Add sugar, ketchup, salt, white pepper, cayenne, Worcestershire, bitters, and food coloring.

3. Make a blond roux with the butter and flour. Blend well into the greens, until the sauce takes on a different, lighter texture. Then mix in the bread crumbs.

4. Place large, fresh oysters into oyster shells, small ovenproof rame-kins, or small au gratin dishes. Top each oyster with a generous tablespoon of sauce (or more, if you like). Bake fifteen minutes, or until the top of the sauce has barely begun to brown. Serve immediately.

Note: If you bake oysters using oyster shells, serve on a bed of rock salt or a napkin to keep the shells from rocking.

SERVES EIGHT.

Red Snapper Basilico

This is one of the most popular fish dishes at Andrea's, and one of the best, too. The sauce is light but complex, with understated herbal flavors. My favorite match for the basilico sauce is red snapper, but it works with almost any white fish. The recipe comes from *La Cucina di Andrea's*, the cookbook I wrote with chef Andrea Apuzzo in the 1980s.

Fish Marinade

¼ cup extra-virgin olive oil

¼ cup dry white wine

1 Tbs. lemon juice

½ tsp. Worcestershire sauce

Dash Tabasco

Fish

4 red snapper fillets, 8 to 10 oz. each

Salt and pepper

Trace flour

¼ cup vegetable oil

3 Tbs. extra-virgin olive oil

3 Tbs. onion, chopped

2 tsp. garlic, chopped

½ cup fresh tomatoes, peeled, seeds removed, and cut into small cubes

⅔ cup dry white wine

½ cup fish stock

1 Tbs. small capers

1 tsp. lemon juice

¼ tsp. Worcestershire sauce

¼ cup fresh mushrooms, sliced

4 Tbs. fresh basil leaves, chopped

1 Tbs. Italian parsley, chopped

1. Wash the fish under cold water, and pat dry. Mix all marinade ingredients together. Marinate the fish for a minute or two on each side. Sprinkle the fillets lightly with salt, pepper, and flour.

2. Heat the vegetable oil in a large sauté pan over medium heat. Put

two fillets of snapper at a time into the pan, and cook three to five minutes per side, until the exterior of the fish is crusty. Remove the fish from the pan, and keep warm.

3. Pour out the remaining vegetable oil, but don't clean the pan. Add and heat the extra-virgin olive oil over medium heat. Sauté the onion and garlic until lightly browned around the edges.

4. Stir in the tomatoes, heat through, and then add the white wine. Bring to a boil, then add the fish stock, capers, lemon juice, and Worcestershire. Return to a boil and reduce by about half, over low heat.

5. Add mushrooms and heat through. Add basil and parsley. Add salt and pepper to taste. Nap the hot sauce over the fish, and serve immediately.

SERVES FOUR.

Ragout of Mushrooms with Grits

Prepared in a ragout, mushrooms achieve a much more intense flavor than they would if simply sautéed in butter. As for the mushrooms, standard white ones are fine, but it's better to mix in some wild species.

Grits
2 cups half-and-half
½ tsp. salt
¾ cup grits, preferably Anson Mills stone-ground white grits
2 Tbs. butter
Ragout
1 stick butter
6 Tbs. flour

2 Tbs. onions, chopped
½ square (½ oz.) Baker's dark chocolate
¾ cup half-and-half
½ cup warm, strong beef stock or broth
½ cup port, Madeira, or Marsala wine
16 oz. assorted mushrooms, cleaned and sliced into pieces the
    size of garlic cloves
¼ tsp. marjoram
1 tsp. Worcestershire sauce
½ tsp. salt
3 dashes Tabasco chipotle-pepper sauce
Salt and pepper

1. Make the grits first by bringing the half-and-half and the salt to a light boil. Stir in the grits, and lower the heat to the lowest temperature. Cook, stirring now and then, until a furrow you make drawing a spoon across the surface remains for a few seconds. Remove from the heat. Let the butter melt on top of the hot grits, and tilt the pan around to coat the surface with butter (don't stir it in). Keep the grits warm, covered, in an oven at the lowest setting.

2. For the ragout, melt the butter in a saucepan over medium heat, and add the flour. Make a light brown roux, stirring constantly until the mixture reaches the color of a brown paper bag. Add the onions and the chocolate, and remove from the heat. Continue to stir until the chocolate fully melts.

3. Whisk in the half-and-half until the mixture takes on the texture of mashed potatoes. Whisk in the beef stock and the wine until well blended. Add the remaining ingredients, and lower the heat to the lowest temperature. Cover and cook for about fifteen minutes, stirring every now and then, until the mixture is very thick and the mushrooms are very soft. Adjust salt and pepper to taste.

4. Stir in that butter on top of the grits, and spoon onto plates. Surround or top the grits (at your discretion) with the mushroom ragout. Serve with steak, roast beef, roast pork, or lamb leg.

SERVES SIX TO EIGHT.

PART TWO

The World Before the Storm

The front of Emeril's, an adaptive use of a warehouse.

CHAPTER SIX

The Stars Come Out

EMERIL, SUSAN, AND RICHARD

The balance of power in newsworthy New Orleans restaurants shifted from the front of the house to the back on March 26, 1990. That was opening day for Emeril's, the most eagerly awaited new dining establishment in New Orleans history. After two days of shakedown dinners for friends and colleagues (and nine-month-old Jude Fitzmorris), the buzz harmonized into a hum, and the whole city was talking about the place.

Emeril told me that the best comment he heard on those two nights came from his ex-boss, Ella Brennan, who cheered him on when he left Commander's to open his own place. On his opening night, her advice was "Change nothing!"

Emeril's restaurant was a complete departure from Commander's Palace. There, the Brennans and others wearing suits in the front of the house were in charge. All things being equal, the Brennans and their managers had the last say on how things would go down in any controversy in the kitchen. That was true even though none of the Brennans, by their own admission, were chefs. Emeril's, on the other hand, was by definition an expression of the will of the chef. Emeril would dress in whites, not a suit. It was the chef that the customers wanted to visit their tables, not the maître d'.

Emeril's was hardly the first chef-owned restaurant in New Orleans, but even the best of those that had come before—like LeRuth's, La Provence, and Crozier's—were modest operations. In inexpensive facilities in suburban neighborhoods, chef-owners ran their restaurants out of their back pockets. No big support staffs, outside investors, or large loans. They could succeed by just serving local regulars, and they didn't have to worry about attracting tourists and conventioneers.

But Emeril's was a major undertaking in a prime location, with a very large staff. I got a clue as to how big a deal it was when the bank that was considering underwriting the project called me. "Could a mere chef manage so ambitious a restaurant?" was the essence of the question. I told the banker that if there were any chef who could, it was Emeril Lagasse. You couldn't talk to the guy without feeling his magnetism. To eat his food was to love him. And nobody who hung on at the top for seven years with Ella and Dick Brennan could possibly be ignorant of how to make a restaurant successful.

The bank had nothing to worry about. Emeril's was a slam dunk from opening day. And, unlike most new restaurants, it didn't experience a post-honeymoon decline. It's still on a roll, almost twenty years later.

The most compelling aspect of Emeril's was the supremacy of the chef and his food. This ran counter to the established experience in big-deal restaurants. It wasn't just an illusion; you could step up and watch Emeril and his chefs cooking, since the entrée station was behind an open food bar. If you dined at the bar, you would see your food being prepared a few feet in front of you.

All of this was novel and fascinating to the sensibilities of younger diners. To them, the idea that cooking took precedence over dining room formalities made sense. It was the gourmet bistro idea again, bounced upscale. And it was cool, to boot.

The quick and impressive success of Emeril's first restaurant opened the door to other chefs to move into the spotlight. Within a few months, two other major chef-managed restaurants opened. Like Emeril's, they quickly had packed houses, which have rarely relented to this day.

Susan Spicer was one of the young chefs who powered the Uptown gourmet bistro boom in the early 1980s. She is also one of my 500 People. The last job she had before she started cooking professionally was as a typesetter for my *New Orleans Menu*. (I am not claiming that she received even a little of her inspiration or ability from that experience.)

After spending some time in France, Susan returned to New Orleans as chef at the Bistro at the Maison de Ville—a new, tiny, and excellent hotel restaurant that would become famous for hiring great chefs on their way up. That certainly described Susan. Less than a week after Emeril's premiered, she opened Bayona in an atmospheric old French Quarter building. She had partners, but there was no mistaking that Chef Spicer (what a great name!) was in charge.

Susan cooks in a style so personal that it defies labeling. (Since one of my jobs is coming up with those labels, I say this with some assurance.) She puts more emphasis on ingredients than techniques, spending a lot of time hunting down unusually good foodstuffs. When she opened Bayona, this made for unique menus. Instead of naming dishes in the standard way—Salmon Bayona, say—she had Pacific Wild-caught Salmon with Choucroute and Gewurztraminer Sauce. It was like a minirecipe. That sort of thing is the rule now, but it was uncommon then.

Susan also reached out more than most chefs of the time did. She was (and still is) visibly involved in the community, particularly in antihunger and women's charities. She cultivated a network of local farmers and artisan food producers long before most other New Orleans chefs did. She encouraged people working for her to step out and be noticed, both in her own restaurant and in the ones they would open on their own. Most restaurateurs in those days would do all they could to keep their employees from breaking away; Susan did the opposite. For example, she helped Donald Link, one of her former sous-chefs, to open Herbsaint. It was a big enough hit that he has since opened two other spots, including the phenomenal post-Katrina Cochon.

Susan's low-key personality wouldn't lead to the stardom that the ebullient Emeril naturally fell into. But there's no question that she is one of the best-liked people in the New Orleans restaurant community. You never hear a bad word about her, and hardly ever about her restaurant.

Four months after Bayona opened and four blocks away, Richard

COOKING WITH CHEF AMETHYST

With no limits imposed on the type or length of my articles for The New Orleans
Menu Daily, *I tried a lot of new ideas. This was one of the most eccentric. Alleged to
be a weekly cooking class from one chef Amethyst LeSolide, it was a parody loosely
based on Emeril Lagasse and his new approach to restaurant cooking. Chef Amethyst
took Emeril's ideas to absurd extremes. The series appeared every Monday in the newsletter for months, but the chef never got to the end of the first recipe.*

Lesson 1: Grillades and Grits

How you guys doin'? Maybe your mother or grandmother made grillades and
grits, and I'll bet they were terrific. That cheap veal with the bones still on
tasted great after it had been cooked with canned tomato paste and the ever-
present Holy Trinity (onions, celery, and bell peppers) for hours and hours in
that same big old pot she used for everything.

I'll bet that great old dish would be even better if your grandma had access to
the kind of food and equipment and, let's face it, consciousness that we have
today. Indeed, I found the thought so thrilling that a couple of years ago I created my up-to-date version of grillades and grits for the restaurant.

You'd better get started right away. The first step in the cooking is to brown
off the veal, which is where the flavor in your sauce is going to come from.
This was the first place where I felt a major improvement was in order. The
cheap cuts of veal never quite tasted right, and the aroma was all wrong. I
felt that a lighter, more aromatic meat was needed.

I did what I always do when I can't find what I want in the open market: I get
somebody to produce it to my specifications. I found a farmer in Washington
Parish to raise veal calves fed on nothing but their mother's milk, fresh clover,
and a certain daily amount of rosemary. It was tough getting the calves to eat
the rosemary—the pointy leaves pricked their noses and tasted bitter to them.
We found that the solution was to puree the rosemary with some cream. It
took awhile—I insisted that we use only 50 percent butterfat cream—but we
finally got the little calves to eat it up every morning before they were fully
awake.

When we butchered the calves, I used the veal round from only the left leg.
It's known that veal calves sleep with most of their weight on the right leg.
This makes for a more sinewy meat, and it was my goal to have very tender
veal for my grillades. I recommend that you do all of what I just told you to
make your grillades all they can be.

Once I have the meat in-house, I improve the flavor and texture by slicing the meat exactly three-quarters of an inch thick and slathering it all over with pure parsley-seed oil. I used to buy a breath-freshening product that was mostly parsley-seed oil in gelcaps. I'd break open about fifty gelcaps and collect the oil. But I've since found that it gives the veal a better mouthfeel to use the oil from fresh parsley seeds. You know how strongly I feel about using fresh as opposed to processed products.

For two pounds of veal (that's how much you'll need to make grillades and grits for four), it will require pressing about 30 pounds of parsley seeds to get enough oil to properly coat the meat. The pressing can be done in the same press you use to press olives, peanuts, and cottonseeds for your homemade vegetable oils.

Now, don't think I'm not aware that this is an almost unheard-of amount of parsley seeds, and that it will be hard to get. This is where the relationship with your friendly farmer once again comes in handy. My salvation came from Handy Walford, who farms on the low hills just outside Montpelier, Mississippi. I got him to put in three acres of parsley for me.

The best parsley-seed oil comes from a different variety of parsley than the one that has the best leaves. So after waiting the two years it takes for parsley to go to seed, Handy found himself with a terrific amount of extra parsley leaves on his hands that I simply could not buy. But you have to help a friend like that, so I hooked him up with my rabbit man. We found that rabbits fed a diet of nothing but parsley and parsnips had a taste that was indescribably slightly better than normal.

But I'm getting off the subject. You won't need three acres of parsley. A fifty-by-fifty-foot patch ought to do it. But, as I mentioned, it takes two years for parsley to come to seed, so let's get to it. The first step in planting parsley for oil is to have the right soil. (I made that rhyme so you'll remember it.)

Remember these three words, too: *humus, humus, humus.* Make it the kind with a high content of the droppings from animals with a high-fat diet. Those are the building blocks of your parsley oil.

So let's rush ahead and say you have the parsley oil. Rub the veal all over with it liberally, using the same hand technique you'd use to massage your lover. If you don't know what I mean by that, I'm glad—that means you'll have to learn from scratch, and you'll learn the right way instead of the usual way.

Hughes opened the Pelican Club on Exchange Alley. That's an address suggestive of mystery and subterfuge in the annals of New Orleans history, but it's right in the middle of the most heavily trafficked part of the French Quarter. It's a large restaurant, and Richard used it for all it was worth.

Richard began his cooking career at an Uptown bistro during those fecund early 1980s. He left town to cook Creole food at a New York restaurant called Memphis. There, he made enough money to return home and open the Pelican Club as he thought it should be. In the Pelican Club's early years, chef Chin Ling was Richard's business partner. The two of them created the world's first Creole-Asian fusion menu. It was, naturally, a point of distinction and a grabber of hip young diners.

Even quieter than Susan Spicer, Richard avoids the spotlight. But the Pelican Club has always been one of my favorite places to refer would-be diners looking for a great restaurant flying under the radar. Fame is not required for great eats.

That's three new, phenomenally successful five-star restaurants in four months. It was as exceptional a time as the week the Beatles held all five of the top spots on the pop charts. Something was obviously going on. Soon, it seemed that every chef in town working for a suit was looking for investors. Quite a few found them. Or maybe it was the other way around.

THE AGE OF INGREDIENTS

Emeril's most distinctive idea was to break with the way restaurants had built their menus in the past. Early in his tenure at Commander's, he talked much more about ingredients than about cooking. It was of paramount importance to him that he begin cooking with foodstuffs of unimpeachable excellence.

This was already an article of faith for the Brennans. Jill Rauch, the food buyer at Commander's (and at Brennan's before the family split), was responsible for the superb quality foodstuffs the chefs had on hand. She was also the scourge of food purveyors. Stories are still told about her stringent standards. For example, she'd make crabmeat vendors open each container and turn it upside down onto a plate to prove that it was jumbo lump at the bottom as well as the top. Try to put something over on her more than once, and the supplier would lose the Brennans' business.

Miss Jill (even Ella Brennan calls her that) is legendary among the chefs she worked with. "Nobody knows more about food than Miss Jill," Emeril told me. Paul Prudhomme agrees. For such a martinet, she struck me as the kind of person you'd meet outside of church on Sunday morning. But then I never had to sell crabmeat to her.

Emeril kicked Miss Jill's standards up a notch. He broke down ingredients into their component parts, and improved them at that level. "If we need mayonnaise for something, we make mayonnaise," he told me early in his tenure at Commander's. "With fresh eggs!"

The next thing we knew, Emeril was conducting experiments. Like making his own Worcestershire sauce. He aged it for months in wood barrels at the restaurant. He had something new along those

---

Restaurant de la Tour Eiffel

In 1985, an old restaurant halfway up the Eiffel Tower was found to be causing structural problems and was closed. It was dismantled into 11,000 pieces, packed into containers, and shipped to New Orleans. Chef Daniel Bonnot—noted for creating the first serious classic French restaurant in town—rebuilt the old Eiffel Tower restaurant on St. Charles Avenue. It was brilliant for about a year, then faded and closed.

At its peak, I went to the Eiffel Tower for dessert and Champagne, as the sole date for ten young female models. They'd just put on a show for the Opera Association, whose president asked me to treat the girls to something nice. Chef Daniel made eleven different hot soufflés for us. I don't expect to ever see such a performance again.

The Eiffel Tower was the buzz of the town when it opened, and it was such a good tale that I was able to sell a story and a photograph about it to *Food & Wine*. The place is still standing, after opening and closing as several other restaurants. As of this writing, it's the Cricket Club, a catering hall.

lines for our threesome to try on our First Tuesday dinners almost every month.

Some of it struck me as a pure mind game. Really, is there enough Worcestershire sauce in any dish that making your own would give a noticeable flavor advantage? I wrote a parody of Emeril's obsession with ingredients (see page 98). A fictional chef Amethyst LeSolide wrote about making veal grillades and grits, a classic Creole dish. The recipe began with instructions on raising your own veal calves. Then growing your own tomatoes, after going down to Mexico to get a certain kind of wild seeds. By the seventh installment, Chef Amethyst was mining the metal to make his own saucepans. When I gave it up, not one ingredient had yet begun to cook.

On the other hand, this emphasis on exceptional ingredients brought us New Orleanians many moments of surprised gustatory delight. Emeril was well enough tuned-in that his food never became contrived. He once said, "What I love about people in New Orleans is that to make them happy, you only need to give them food that tastes great. You don't have to mess with their heads, too." (Even though he did, at least a little.)

Much messing with heads was going on in restaurants then. As the mania for unusual ingredients grew, some chefs used them more for effect than for flavor. Sometimes, it seemed to me that they intentionally tried to puzzle their customers. The first chef of a short-lived restaurant called Indigo carried that to an extreme. Every dish included an ingredient I'd never heard of, let alone tasted. If a food writer was mystified, what were average diners making of this stuff? Susan Spicer's highly descriptive menu nomenclature fell prey to a similar trend. At first it became standard among the hipper chefs. Then, as seems inevitable, it went over the edge. Single sprigs of microgreens (the silliest new ingredients of all) and sprinklings of seasonings that could be measured in grains were mentioned. One chef who specified aged balsamic vinegar as a critical ingredient in a dish released a single drop of the stuff onto the plate.

When I interview chefs who play these games, I respond to their dish descriptions as if I were about to expire with delight. They rarely catch on that I am pulling their leg. They really believe that this is cooking. But it isn't. It's contrivance. As well trained and knowledgeable as the new generation of chefs is, some have no idea what tastes good. Nor do they seem to care. All that matters is being able to tell a good backstory.

Alex Patout was one of the few chefs who refused to join the ingredients revolution. He came up from New Iberia in the wake of Paul Prudhomme and ran many restaurants over the years, always emphasizing the rustic nature of Cajun cooking. "Nobody's cooking anymore!" he told me over lunch at Galatoire's. (Alex was one of the few restaurateurs I often ran into in other restaurants.) "They take a slab of tuna or a steak, throw it on the grill, top it with foie gras or crabmeat, put a sprig of fresh thyme next to it, and call it cooking. Who's crunching crab shells and simmering them down for two hours to get the fat anymore? That's what Louisiana cooking is really about!"

I remember what Chef Paul said when he first came to town: "What makes Cajun food great is that for a hundred years we had to sell all our best fish to make a living," he said. "We ate the trash fish ourselves. But we learned how to make it taste good." Traditional Cajun and Creole food takes a lot of time and work. And it takes real cooking.

SOMETHING FISHY

Another current helped launch the Age of Ingredients in New Orleans and pulled us away from our established culinary traditions. The fish population was having problems.

Blackened redfish is often blamed. Chefs all over the country in the 1980s were inspired by Chef Paul's example and added Cajun food to their repertoires. Blackened redfish was the signature dish of that vogue. Not understanding the concept, chefs in other places just followed the recipe, assuming it could only be made with redfish. Since most of them were accustomed to buying frozen fish from far away (where else do you get fish in Denver or Dallas?), they placed their orders. The wholesalers told the fishermen they needed more redfish, and the fishermen obliged.

The demand crashed the redfish population. Fishermen started hauling in "bull reds"—big, tough redfish full of blood lines. Eating these would leave a bad taste in your mouth when it came to redfish and, by extension, Cajun food generally. Worst of all, these large fish being caught up were the breeding stock for the species. So fewer baby redfish were born.

The sport-fishing industry seized on the overfishing to demand that the commercial catch of redfish be stopped; it was something they'd long hoped for, and now they had a good story. Commercial fishermen made good ogres. They were notorious for wiping out populations of fish with the likes of gill nets.

The sport fishermen won. By 1990, redfish was a sport-only fish almost everywhere along the Gulf Coast, from Mexico to Florida, including Louisiana. That meant it could no longer be sold. By anybody. Not by fish markets, restaurants, or wholesalers. So the commercial fishermen, who in many ways were their own worst enemies, moved on to other species. The sport-fishing guys returned to state legislatures with their figures and their lobbying money. One after another, the fish on New Orleans restaurant tables became off-limits to chefs.

A particularly painful example of the process is still going on. Speckled trout is a medium-size, whitish-gray fish that thrives in the brackish waters around New Orleans. For decades it was the most popular fish in New Orleans restaurants, from the fried-seafood houses to the top-of-the-scale joints. Many classic Creole dishes were made for the fish. When redfish became unavailable, demand shifted to speckled trout. The population decreased; the sport-fishing groups called their politicians; and a new law greatly decreased the trout available to restaurants. Now, under the new law, all the restaurants and fish markets are forced to share less than one half of 1 percent of the annual catch of speckled trout. Meaning that unless you catch it yourself, Louisiana speckled trout is today a rare treat, available only in the short season, in late fall and winter.

As a result of all this, the restaurants often found themselves with no local fish to cook. Seafood is so important to New Orleans cuisine that this qualified as a crisis. Fish had to be found somewhere. It began coming from two sources: other parts of the world and fish farms. For the first time ever, salmon began showing up on New Orleans menus. What's the Creole recipe for salmon? There wasn't one, because there was no salmon around until recently. Catfish, traditionally the province of inexpensive cafés, began turning up on white tablecloths.

The advent of the Age of Ingredients actually helped the situation. Customers a few years earlier would not have accepted amberjack, mahi-mahi, grouper, or other newly introduced fish. They now applauded it. That opened the doors to piscine diversity. Today you can find restaurants with a dozen or more species of finfish on their menus every night. That's at least triple what we had in the 1980s.

But the typical New Orleans eater still longs to have redfish and trout in a restaurant again. Especially since the populations of both fish are once again very healthy. Plus, the commercial fishermen have been regulated so stringently for so long now that it's unlikely they'll be able to run amok again.

After Hurricane Katrina, as soon as the fishing boats could be dragged back into the water again (some were found miles inland), they came back with lots of fish, oysters, and shrimp to be cooked. Nobody could believe it, but there it was. Thank God.

Quail with Dried Cherries and Pinot Noir

Susan Spicer is one of New Orleans's most celebrated culinarians. Her imagination is most fertile and tempered by uncommonly accurate good taste. This dish plays the cherrylike aspects of California Pinot Noir wine against real cherries. Dried cherries, which might be a little hard to find, are to cherries what raisins are to grapes. (You could probably get away with using fresh cherries in this recipe.) Susan prepared this dish for a television segment I shot with her at her five-star restaurant Bayona.

> 2 oz. dried cherries
> 1¼ cup Pinot Noir
> 1 French dried shallot, chopped
> 1 sprig fresh tarragon, chopped
> ½ cup strong quail stock, made from bones
> 2 Tbs. currant jelly
> 2 Tbs. butter, softened
> Salt and pepper
> 8 quails, partially deboned
> 10 oz. fresh spinach, well washed and picked over

1. Plump the dried cherries in ¼ cup of the wine for two hours.

2. In a small saucepan, reduce the remaining wine with the shallot and the tarragon to about half its original volume. Add the quail stock and currant jelly. Reduce until somewhat syrupy. Whisk in the butter, and add salt and pepper to taste. Remove from the heat, and keep warm.

3. Season the quails with salt and pepper, and grill or sauté until done—about four minutes, depending on size.

4. With the water clinging to the leaves after washing, wilt the spinach in a large pot over medium heat, keeping a little bit of body.

5. Place the spinach on a plate. Top with two quails per person. Surround the plate with the sauce, then garnish with the plumped cherries, making sure everyone gets a few.

SERVES FOUR.

Seared Scallops with Artichokes

This is a signature dish at the Pelican Club, where chef Richard Hughes calls it by the misleading name Scallop-stuffed Artichoke. Sophisticated in both flavor and appearance, it's best made with dry-pack (aka "day-boat") scallops, which have not been processed for a long shelf life. (The ones in the supermarket are probably not this kind.) Careful: Don't overcook the scallops! Use high heat, and get them out of the pan while they're still bulging.

4 small whole artichokes

Scallops

¼ cup clarified butter

1 lb. sea scallops, medium-large

1 tomato, diced

Garlic Beurre Blanc

1 Tbs. white vinegar

½ cup white wine

1 Tbs. heavy cream

1 head garlic, roasted until semisoft

1½ sticks unsalted butter, softened

Salt and pepper

Vinaigrette

1 Tbs. balsamic vinegar

1 tsp. fresh tarragon

1 Tbs. Italian parsley, chopped

1 tsp. grated Parmesan cheese

¼ cup extra-virgin olive oil

1 tomato, diced

1. Wash and then steam the artichokes until tender—about twenty to thirty minutes. Pull off and save thirty-two perfect leaves. Clean and remove the artichoke bottoms, then save the rest of the artichoke parts for another use.

2. For the garlic beurre blanc, bring the vinegar and wine to a boil in a skillet. Lower the heat to almost nothing, and add the heavy

cream. Puree the garlic (don't use a garlic press), and add to the pan. Slowly whisk in the softened butter, then add salt and pepper to taste. Remove from heat and reserve.

3. Heat one-third of the clarified butter in a skillet over medium-high heat. Sauté the sea scallops until lightly browned, but still bulging—about a minute and a half per side. Add more butter to the pan as necessary to complete the cooking.

4. Combine all the ingredients for the vinaigrette, whisking the oil slowly into the other ingredients.

5. Place an artichoke bottom on each plate. Surround it with eight artichoke leaves. Drizzle some vinaigrette over the artichokes. Divide the scallops among the four plates, and spoon 2 Tbs. garlic beurre blanc over each. Garnish with diced tomato.

SERVES FOUR.

RECIPE

Marinated Shrimp with Artichokes

Louisiana white shrimp appear in late summer and fall. I believe they are the world's best shrimp. Here's a chilled shrimp dish that qualifies, I suppose, as a Creole antipasto. It's pretty good as is, served chilled. Or you can toss it with greens or with cooked, chilled pasta as a salad.

Sauce
½ cup Creole mustard or another coarse-grained brown mustard
2 eggs
½ Tbs. salt
⅓ tsp. red bell pepper, finely chopped
1 cup vegetable oil

¼ cup tarragon vinegar
1 cup green onion, chopped
¾ cup chives, chopped
¾ cup parsley, chopped
Shrimp
2 Tbs. salt
Juice of half a lemon
1 Tbs. liquid crab boil
2 lbs. medium to large shrimp, peeled

2 cans artichoke hearts, drained and quartered

1. Prepare the sauce. Mix the mustard, eggs, salt, and red pepper together in a food processor. (You can also use a wire whisk in a bowl.) Add the vegetable oil a few drops at a time, while continuing to blend the egg mixture. When the mixture begins to thicken, increase the addition of oil to a thin stream. Blend until well mixed. Add the vinegar, green onions, chives, and parsley.

2. Bring one quart of water to a rolling boil in a saucepan, with the salt, lemon juice, and crab boil. After the seasoned water has boiled for three minutes, add the shrimp. When the water returns to a boil, turn off the heat, and allow the shrimp to steep in the water for about four minutes—until they're pink and firm. (When you first wonder whether the shrimp are cooked, that's when they are.) Strain out the shrimp, and allow them to cool for a few minutes.

3. In a large bowl, mix the shrimp and the artichokes into the sauce. Cover the bowl, and put it into the refrigerator to marinate for at least an hour. Serve shrimp tossed with salad greens, tomatoes, or chilled pasta—or all by itself.

MAKES EIGHT APPETIZERS.

Chez Helene, the first predominantly black restaurant many white Orleanians (including me) ever set foot in. *The Underground Gourmet* turned us on to it. It was in back of the grocery store where my mother shopped when we lived six blocks away from the place.
©1978 Christopher R. Harris.

CHAPTER SEVEN

Localism Leads to Cuisine

SLEAZY CHIC

The office of the *Figaro* newspaper, where I worked throughout the 1970s, was within walking distance of a dumpy old neighborhood café called Uglesich's. It was one of many Croatian-owned restaurants that opened around New Orleans between the wars—1924 in this case. Uglesich's was primarily a poor boy sandwich shop. It was better than most, because it had an oyster bar. (Croatian settlers in Louisiana have long dominated the oyster trade.) Uglesich's not only fried the oysters to order for your sandwich, but shucked them to order, too.

Anthony Uglesich, the second-generation owner, felt no urgency about making changes to his dad's restaurant. He deferred painting the place for a span of years during which most people would have painted it two or three times. The ventilation system was so ineffective that when we returned from lunch at Uglesich's, nobody had to ask where we'd been; we smelled as if we'd been frying fish all day. When I touted the place's virtues to radio listeners, they sometimes called back to say that they'd gone there, but when they saw the place they just kept driving.

Uglesich's was deteriorating in step with its neighborhood. The grand pre–Civil War houses were coming down one by one. Sometimes by demolition, sometimes by gravity. The lots were usually left vacant, and the area looked more distressed and forbidding with each passing year.

Lunch business from the big Brown's Velvet Dairy across the street kept Uglesich's going. A host of unique characters—some of whom appeared in newspaper articles or on television once in a while, as examples of local color—hung around the place all day long. When the *Figaro* staff went to Uglesich's, we found a restaurant most New Orleanians had forsaken, if they knew about it at all. We, of course, loved it. Uglesich's was what we meant by our editorial motto, "Localism alone leads to culture."

Around 1985, it suddenly became impossible to get a table at Uglesich's. The dining room—still in need of a paint job, still aromatic with frying oysters—was filled up at all hours, every day. Not only with local people but tourists. Tourists at Uglesich's! How did they find the place? Major celebrities visiting New Orleans somehow turned up there. Some of those would buy out the place for an evening and hold big parties attended by other celebrities. The *Figaro* gang and other longtime Uglesich's customers thought this newfound currency hilarious. Uglesich's was the same old place it had always been. The only new development was that Anthony and his wife Gail had begun cooking a few daily-plate specials to add to the poor boys and seafood platters. Those were good, but not enough to explain the new phenomenon.

For the next twenty years, Uglesich's became for many people the ultimate expression of what eating in New Orleans was about. Its fame spread among fans of New Orleans food throughout the country. Flush with this success, Anthony finally performed a light renovation. He replaced some of the old fixtures, built a new kitchen, fixed the exhaust system, and even painted. The customers were wary of all this gussying up, but got used to it.

Uglesich's fame and volume increased right up until the day in 2005 when Anthony and Gail retired and closed the restaurant. It was right after the Jazz Festival in early May, which brought in customers by the horde. (That was also a few months before Hurricane Katrina, which the old joint survived without serious damage.) During the spot's final weeks, the line of customers extended out the door and far down the sidewalk. Then Uglesich's closed. But it didn't die. The Uglesich family has published two cookbooks of its recipes since the last time the restaurant was open. Every few days, an excited correspondent asks me whether there's any truth to the ever-circulating rumor that Uglesich's will reopen.

The best description of the Uglesich phenomenon came from a late *Figaro* colleague, Don Lee Keith. He called it "sleazy chic." He wasn't writing about Uglesich's at the time, but generally about the taste our city has for the seedy, the raffish, the seamy, the greasy, the smelly, the decadent, the yeasty, the worn-out, and the cheap. For reasons rarely borne out by reality, we believe that sleazy chic coincides with authentic local pleasure. No better example of sleazy chic existed than Uglesich's.

New Orleans has long had a reputation as being one of the most cultured and sophisticated cities in the United States. It had the first opera house in America and was so sympathetic to artists of all stripes that it attracted many of them to move to town. Articles and guidebooks from the 1960s and before stressed words like *genteel* and showed pictures of neighborhoods like the Garden District. Most locals thought about the city that way, too—even locals who were poor and lived in funky neighborhoods.

In the years following World War II, while Europe was still largely destroyed, New Orleans became a primary destination for Americans who wanted to enjoy advanced, ambitious cuisine. Those gourmets didn't come to town to go to the likes of Uglesich's, or even century-old seafood houses like Bruning's on Lake Pontchartrain. They came to dress up and dine grandly at Antoine's, Arnaud's, Galatoire's, Broussard's, and perhaps the upstart Brennan's.

Orleanians of those days, from the top of the income scale to the lower middle, had their own favorite restaurants in their own favorite price ranges. Neighborhood cafés were within walking distance of wherever you lived in the city's established neighborhoods. All of them had a certain decorum and made at least an attempt at décor, to give the feeling that one was stepping out. They even served some of the same dishes that the big, famous places in the French Quarter did—just not as fancily.

Lower-income people—my family, for example—hardly went to restaurants at all. My mother cooked delicious, distinctive Creole food at home and never took a day off from that project. When my Uncle Billy took me to Clarence and Lefty's for that memorable roast beef poor boy in 1961, it was my first visit to any kind of restaurant. The qualities that would coalesce into sleazy chic were there all along, of course. Seedy cafés, bars, and music clubs in dumpy, smoky, smelly old dives on backstreets were all over New Orleans. Until the 1970s, for many Orleanians all this could just as well have

Top New Orleans Restaurants, 1992

These ratings came from an update to *The New Orleans Eat Book*, the most encyclopedic restaurant guide I ever published. The new wave of major chef-owned restaurants was well under way at the time. The bolded restaurants are still open as of 2010. The entire book from which these ratings came is available to read online: http://www. nomenu.com/EatBook

★★★★★ FIVE STARS ★★★★★
(the maximum rating)

Andrea's
Bayona
Commander's Palace
Crozier's
Emeril's
La Provence
Mr. B's Bistro
Pelican Club
Versailles
Windsor Court Grill Room

★★★★ FOUR STARS ★★★★

Antoine's	Lafitte's Landing
Arnaud's	Le Jardin
Bistro at the Maison de Ville	Louis XVI
Bozo's	**Morton's**
Brennan's	**Mosca's**
Brigtsen's	**Nuvolari's**
Christian's	Peking
Clancy's	**Ruth's Chris**
DiPiazza's	**Sal & Judy's**
El Patio	**Trey Yuen**
Flagons	**Tujague's**
Galatoire's	**Upperline**
Gambrill's	Young's Steak House
Gautreau's	
Ichiban	
La Cuisine	

been quarantined, or even torn down to make way for something nicer. Then *Figaro* and its baby boomer readers began to seek out and glorify the best of these low-down local pleasures: Local music, food, and architecture were the major subjects of this renaissance.

Sleazy chic left a lasting mark on the local culture, including its food. By the 1990s, it was considered gospel that the "real" New Orleans flavor was not to be found in restaurants like Commander's Palace or Emeril's anymore, but in the likes of Uglesich's. Sleazy chic joints found their popularity swelling unexpectedly.

It happened just in the nick of time. Even as nostalgia grew for the old neighborhood restaurants, it was discovered that they were endangered. The culprit was the national chain restaurant. Fast-food "stores" (to use the soulless industry jargon) nabbed many of the customers who formerly went to the neighborhood cafés when they didn't feel like cooking. For every new McDonald's or Kentucky Fried Chicken that opened in town, two neighborhood restaurants died. Because the cafés were usually hidden on the corner of a side street and another side street, few people other than the neighbors noticed the attrition.

The few survivors were those lucky enough to have visible locations. Mandina's was the most celebrated. Its distinctive neon signs got everybody's attention on busy Canal Street in Mid-City. Its menu is a neighborhood restaurant classic: gumbo and turtle soup; fried seafood; poor boys; fried chicken; an Italian section; and good daily home-style Creole specials, recurring predictably. The ingredients were never the best, but the prices were low, and the portions enormous. It was always a full house.

"Tell me about a good hole-in-the-wall restaurant in my neighborhood; you know, a place like Mandina's." That was the top request on my radio show those days. The callers honestly believed such restaurants existed and that it was just a matter of finding them. When I said that no corner cafés existed anymore where they lived, they often didn't believe me. They accused me of keeping secrets and didn't like my saying, "If you like places like Mandina's, go to Mandina's." Whenever I did find a good unknown neighborhood spot, it was usually of very recent vintage. With the old neighborhood restaurants gone, many new ones opened to serve the reawakened customers. Most were a bit too intent on re-creating nostalgia, but they were often better than the restaurants they were imitating—the result of our raised culinary consciousness from the gourmet Creole bistro and the ingredients age.

Some chefs saw in this an interesting opportunity. What if they served the food of the gourmet bistros, but in the premises of a neighborhood joint? Such restaurants became wildly successful, rivaling the Uglesich's phenomenon.

Voodoo Gourmet

The archetype of that genre is Jacques-Imo's. Jack Leonardi, a New York native, came to town to attend Tulane. On the side, he worked in the kitchen at K-Paul's. He loved New Orleans food, knew how to cook, and had an outsider's perspective on what made New Orleans food special. In 1996, he bought an ancient poor boy shop in the old Oak Street commercial district Uptown and began serving sandwiches and platters. He persuaded Austin Leslie—one of the two or three most famous black Creole chefs—to come out of retirement and prepare his legendary fried chicken at Jacques-Imo's.

For the first year or so, a meal at Jacques-Imo's usually began when Jack came over to your table, sat down, and asked you what you felt like eating. He'd cook almost anything you wanted, with the ingredients he had in house. As he settled in, he built a menu of the greatest hits of contemporary New Orleans and Cajun cookery. K-Paul's–style eats were mixed with other popular dishes, all served on ramshackle premises that included a bumpy courtyard in the back and an open kitchen in the middle. It was all decorated with voodoo candles and other funky old New Orleans stuff. Local R&B and jazz played in the background.

To me, Jacques-Imo's (the name is a corruption of a line from an old Mardi Gras street chant) is a caricature of New Orleans food and culture. But I plead a handicap. Unlike most of the other customers, who skew to the younger end of the age spectrum and take the place at face value, I have firsthand experience with the original versions of most of the culinary and atmospheric elements that Jack cuts and pastes into his restaurant. But there are plenty enough

patrons around to fill Jacques-Imo's densely. You need a sh
a crowbar, and a jar of Vaseline to get into the place most
Jacques-Imo's is to those customers the essence of the authentı
Orleans restaurant, with all the sleazy chicness they crave.

Another runaway success along the same lines is Dick and
Jenny's. Dick Benz was the chef first for Gautreau's and then for
the Upperline, two of the most stable and best of the original 1983
class of Uptown gourmet Creole bistros. He had his eye on an old
neighborhood bar on Tchoupitoulas Street, the main drag along the
wharf-lined industrial riverfront. When he saw the place up for sale,
he bought it. He and his wife Jenny cleaned, painted, and repaired,
but they did not exactly renovate the place. The look is strictly from
the funky part of town.

Dick's food was like what he'd cooked before but with an interesting difference. He didn't buy much of the expensive, rare food
that Emeril, Jamie, and Susan were cooking. He did, however, stay
with fresh, local foodstuffs, of which there is much around New
Orleans, particularly in the seafood department. Reflecting this
choice of ingredients were prices noticeably lower than those of the
gourmet bistros.

In the sleazy chic age, that was a magical combination. Delicious,
hip, local food at lower-than-normal prices, served in an old heap
of a place? Perfect. Customers suspended whatever doubt they may
have had about the precise grade of the beef and finer points of service. They put up with the major inconvenience of not being able to
reserve tables. Nobody seemed to mind waiting an hour or more to
be seated.

In both the neighborhood and gourmet versions of sleazy chic
restaurants, dress codes vanished. T-shirt and shorts? No problem. Other downscale trends appealed, too. You would usually
spend less than you would in the more substantial restaurants. You
could go on the spur of the moment, because few sleazy chic spots
accepted reservations.

Having a more formal style than most people I know (I am, for
example, the only person in our six-station on-air staff who rou-
tinely broadcasts in a jacket and tie), I was disturbed by this laxity.
I still tell anyone who will listen that dressing for dinner makes the

experience more pleasurable. For a long time, I thought the pendulum would swing the other way. But sleazy chic locked in as the bedrock style of dining in New Orleans. It will remain so for a long time. And the bedrock is very, very deep in these parts, covered by a lot of river silt.

The final blow to formality was the breakout of "Katrina casual" following the hurricane. All restaurants dropped their dress codes, with only one exception. At Galatoire's, a jacket (but no longer a tie) is still required of men at dinner. The food and service went over to sleazy chic, too. But more on that later.

DOWNHEAVAL

"I never go to any Brennan restaurant anymore. I think they're all totally overrated."

I should have known it was coming. But still, it took me aback the first time I heard that on my radio show. Since I was the guy who gave out the ratings, this denigration was not only something I disagreed with, but a challenge to the quality of my research and my pretense of authority. As the 1990s headed to a close, that statement and others like it were voiced more and more often. The one that completely shocked me was this: "What's the big deal about Susan Spicer, anyway? I went to her restaurant and thought the place was snooty."

What? Susan Spicer, snooty? The most likable chef in town, the one with the big heart, who was always raising money for hunger charities, who kept the prices in her five-star restaurant far lower than she could have, who supported local farmers and artisan cheese and bread producers, who had the reputation of being a hip, creative chef, and whose restaurant wasn't yet a decade old? Soft-spoken, lovely Susan Spicer? What could a diner possibly find snooty about her?

The answer, of course, was that her restaurant Bayona was not sleazy chic. Susan executed meticulous cooking with unusual ingredients and boasted a menu full of dishes you never thought about before, served by knowledgeable servers in a beautiful dining room, backed up by a great wine list. You had to make a reservation to dine there; you would not show up in a T-shirt and shorts. But sleazy chic was no longer just a cool thing to have; it was essential if a restaurant wanted local customers. Or hip visitors.

It was hard to believe what was happening. Large numbers of local diners, from baby boom age down, deserted an entire range of restaurants. Antoine's completely fell out of favor with them. Emeril's was being taken over by tourists, now that its chef was famous. Unless a major convention was in town, you could walk into Commander's Palace and get a table. The most astonishing development of all was the dwindling of the line of customers in front of Galatoire's. The line still formed on Fridays at lunch and other times favored by the regulars, but there were days when you could walk right in and sit right down, even at noon or seven in the evening.

We all heard the waiters at Galatoire's complaining about the downturn. But few knew about a deeper unrest behind the scenes. The extended Galatoire family—after a century, it included a lot of people—was not happy with its dwindling profits. Their disturbance grew into a coup, which was instigated sub rosa by Chris Ansel, a third-generation Galatoire. He had left Galatoire's twenty years before to open his own excellent restaurant, Christian's. He and the other Galatoire cousins, aunts, and uncles had always allowed a small number of their relatives to run the restaurant. But in 1997 they rose up and took over. They shocked the community by hiring a nonfamily manager, who held veto power over the existing family management.

Melvin Rodrigue was a young former hotel food-and-beverage manager, who proved to have more on the ball than most people supposed. But his style was more goal-oriented than Galatoire's traditional laissez-faire one. He announced, to a gasping public, that the old restaurant would be thoroughly renovated. That would result in, among other things, the reopening of the second-floor dining rooms for the first time in sixty years.

Galatoire's is such a cherished New Orleans social institution that this news upset a lot of people. The primary article of faith held by the restaurant's regulars was that Galatoire's should never change. Well, here was this Melvin guy changing all kinds of things. He fired a waiter a lot of customers liked. The campaign to get the waiter back spawned a Web site and stories in the national news. The introduction of ice machines, replacing the blocks of ice that had been chiseled with ice picks at Galatoire's since the Cretaceous, occurred just before the new regime took over. But that was blamed on Melvin, too. It may have been the silliest controversy of all. The reaction to the Block Ice Massacre was as if a drive-through had been added to the antique Bourbon Street facade.

The furor kicked up by the changes at Galatoire's was so intense that a book was written about it. Writers Kenneth Holditch and Marda Burton, themselves longtime Galatoire's regulars, wrote *Galatoire's: Biography of a Bistro*. It left only one stone unturned in its analysis of the restaurant and what had happened: It said nothing about how the changes in dining habits wrought by sleazy chic affected every restaurant in New Orleans. Even Galatoire's.

The renovation of Galatoire's was lengthy, thorough, and a tour de force. While few regulars embraced the new upstairs dining rooms, they did like their effects. Tourists who eat up there free up tables for the regulars in the noisy, mirrored, bright, convivial, iconic downstairs main room. Plus, the bar upstairs is a much more comfortable place to wait for a table than out on the sidewalk in the heat, rain, and sun.

It's unlikely that even the most militant opponents of the modernization of Galatoire's would want it to return to the way it was. If pressed, however, they will moan a litany of declines, like the replacement of nonpasteurized crabmeat with pasteurized (but fresh) jumbo lump. And the block ice thing. But after all the updates were in place, Galatoire's was serving more diners than ever before. The hubbub attracted the interest of people who would otherwise have been unlikely to dine there—including a lot of adherents of sleazy chic, who found a certain attractive sleaziness in all the discord.

Corn Macquechoux

Macquechoux is the Cajun-French rendition of a word used by the Native Americans who lived in what is now Louisiana. It meant "cooked corn," but there's much more to it. The corn is cooked down with all the ingredients of a Creole sauce and a lot of butter. This side dish can be turned into an entrée by adding crawfish tails, small shrimp, or diced andouille sausage to the mix about ten minutes before the end of cooking.

    5 ears fresh yellow corn
    1 stick butter
    ½ cup onions, chopped
    1 small red bell pepper, chopped
    1 rib celery, chopped
    2 small, ripe but firm tomatoes, seeds and pulp removed, chopped
    ½ tsp. salt
    ½ tsp. black pepper
    ¼ tsp. cayenne
    Tabasco jalapeno sauce to taste

1. Shuck the corn, and rinse with cold water. Hold the corn upright, with the tip of the ear on a shallow plate. With a sharp knife, cut the kernels off the ear. Use the knife to scrape the ears to extract as much of the corn "milk" as possible. Do this for all the ears.

2. In a medium saucepan, over medium heat, heat the butter until it bubbles, and add the onions, bell pepper, and celery. Cook until the vegetables soften.

3. Lower the heat. Add the corn and the corn milk, and all the other ingredients up to and including the cayenne. Cover and cook, stirring every few minutes, for twenty to twenty-five minutes. If the mixture becomes so dry that it's hard to stir, add a little half-and-half to loosen it up.

4. Add Tabasco jalapeno sauce and additional salt to taste.

MAKES EIGHT SIDE DISHES OR FOUR ENTRÉES.

The New Orleans Eat Book, my most extensive restaurant guide, from 1991.

CHAPTER EIGHT

Good-bye, Creole World

THE CLASS OF 2001

Owen Brennan once said that New Orleans is the boomtown that never booms. Just when the city seems primed for a huge economic expansion, something goes wrong. But the opposite is also true. When the rest of the country is in a crisis, New Orleans is often somehow exempt.

The last years of the 1990s were extraordinarily good to New Orleans. The new convention center brought in record numbers of meetings and trade shows, creating a demand for new hotels and restaurants. And it kept on going into the 2000s, even during the post-9/11 recession.

If my radio show is a gauge of the health of the restaurant business, the dining scene was in great shape indeed in 2002. On a typical program, I was ad-libbing more than twenty commercials. We were usually sold out of advertising airtime, and that was a first for WSMB in quite a while. A lot of this growth came from new restaurants eager to establish themselves. The chef-dominant restaurants kept coming, and they were more image-conscious than their predecessors. Every serious restaurant needed a chef who was not only able to cook and innovate, but who was also attractive and well-spoken.

Even old restaurants with menus set in stone, found young new chefs to front their kitchens. Galatoire's, for example, didn't really have a person who could be called a chef during most of its history. I once wrote a story about that, and I interviewed one of the key men in the kitchen, Charlie Plough. "Before I start talking to you, I want to tell you that I am not a chef!" he said. "I am a cook! That's it!"

That's how all the others there felt, too.

After Melvin Rodrigue arrived, though, Galatoire's had chefs. Brian Landry, the chef as of 2009, is a young guy whose entire career is an almost insignificant fraction of those of the longtime just-plain cooks at Galatoire's. But he had the culinary school background, and he could talk.

Many of these media-friendly chefs had a problem, however. They could make their cooking sound intriguing, but the flavor wasn't there. It was easy to see why. Despite having the best command of technique and knowledge of ingredients in the history of American chefs, they didn't know what tasted good. Sounds good and tastes good are two different things.

Despite their posturing as thoroughly creative, a lot of the new chefs aped current trends from prominent chefs around New Orleans and elsewhere. Instead of serving oysters Rockefeller like everybody else in the old days, they were serving braised pork belly like everybody else in the new days.

But some of the new faces were both pretty and in possession of talented palates. In 2001 came the best crop of major new restaurants since the year of Emeril, Susan, and Richard. Three of the chefs who opened major new restaurants in 2001 came from the same source: the kitchen of the Windsor Court Grill Room. The Grill Room was the best of the grand hotel dining rooms that opened in advance of the 1984 World's Fair, and the only one to survive long-term.

John Besh, Scott Boswell, and Bingo Starr were in the five-star Grill Room kitchen in the mid-1990s, the all-time peak for that establishment. They all left town for a while, but when they returned they each opened their own restaurants.

Besh was the first to make a big splash. In 1999 he had made the cover of *Food & Wine* magazine as one of the top new chefs in the country. At the time, he was the chef of Artesia, an outrageously misplaced restaurant in the lazy little town of Abita Springs. Artesia was within walking distance of my home. I think I may have been the only nearby customer whose tastes fit Artesia's ambitions.

Good-looking (my wife is in love with him) and well-spoken, Besh was the protégé of Chris Kerageorgiou, the presiding genius at La Provence, before opening Artesia. La Provence was enough of a favorite of New Orleans gourmets that they'd make the forty-mile drive to the pine woods of the North Shore to dine there. (It had five of my stars, too.) Besh also spent a month or more in France every year honing his skills. As if all that weren't enough, he was a Marine sergeant who saw action in Kuwait during the first Gulf War. It's hard not to like the guy.

After his success at Artesia, Besh toyed with the idea of opening his own place. Instead, he took an offer to be a partner in a restaurant across the street from the Windsor Court. It opened less than a month after 9/11, but his celebrity was such that the place filled up almost from the outset. A few years later—by which time more than a few people were declaring Restaurant August the best in New Orleans—he bought out his partner. Besh has been on an upward trajectory ever since, and as of this writing has four restaurants, with another in the works.

In the same league as Besh is Scott Boswell. And he has enough of an eccentric streak that his restaurants and food are delightfully quirky. When he opened Stella! (named for the character in *A Streetcar Named Desire*), nobody could figure out where he was going with it. French, Creole, Italian, and Asian flavors came together on the menu, and sometimes even in individual dishes. At a typical meal there, I'll hear someone at another table actually break out in laughter at the waiter's descriptions of certain dishes. Which can indeed get outlandish. Boswell's taste is very sure, however, and his food is solidly in the five-star category. In late 2008, he opened a second restaurant: a drugstore-style soda fountain and lunch counter in the historic lower Pontalba apartment building, one of a matched pair of buildings that flank Jackson Square. In counterpoint to Stella! it's called Stanley.

The third Windsor Court alumnus to open a new major restaurant in 2001 (technically it was late 2000, but close enough) was Richard "Bingo" Starr. He was the chef for the first few years at Cuvée, a restaurant whose theme was new to New Orleans. Co-owner Ken Lacour is a dedicated, world-traveling oenophile, and at his other restaurant, Dakota (another North Shore five-star), built a remarkable cellar. At Cuvée, he planned on selling his customers on a wine program first, then matching up food to the wines, instead of the other way around. That can still be done at Cuvée, which has always maintained a fascinating cellar and one of the city's best tasting menus. When Bob Iacovone replaced Starr as chef, the food became so much better that the wine returned to its traditional supporting role (where it belongs, if you ask me).

The French Direction

August, Stella! and Cuvée were the best new players in the early years of the new millennium. But more major restaurants with headline chefs continued to enhance the restaurant landscape. So many that I couldn't keep up with the new openings. I was very glad for the information flowing in from the radio show and my Web site (which I launched, with a daily e-mail newsletter, in 1996).

French food already loomed large on menus throughout New Orleans restaurant history. It wasn't until the 1990s that the menu at Antoine's was translated into English from the French it had used since opening in 1840. Although the dishes on that menu were so different from the French classics as to make up a regional cuisine—French Creole—the Gallic origins were unmistakable. We had a few more-or-less pure French restaurants, but they were usually in hotels and far behind the curve of current tastes.

In the early 2000s, though, the food of the Parisian and Riviera bistros caught on. Mussels, pâté, onion soup gratiné, bouillabaisse, poulet grand-mère, veal liver Lyonnaise, steak au poivre with pommes frites, tarte Tatin, and all the dishes commonly found with those became a formula for new restaurants. We hadn't seen much of that sort of thing in the past; it went from being nearly unknown to being overexposed in a matter of a few years.

The French bistro food was good, though, and it did add something to the dining possibilities. But I found something disturbing about it. Those restaurants were here not because we were reaching back to our French roots, but because French bistros were in vogue all over the country. Articles about the style were in all the magazines. Anthony Bourdain's memoir *Kitchen Confidential* boosted the style further. Bourdain was then chef at Les Halles, a classic French bistro in Manhattan.

Throughout its history, New Orleans was always a net exporter of culinary innovation; we largely ignored what was going on in other cities around the country. With good reason. Outside New York, San Francisco, and Chicago, no other American city was in a league with New Orleans in its culture of cookery. And not even those cities had so well-developed and old a native flavor as we did. While no restaurant should refrain from serving something delicious just because the idea came from somewhere else, I do think it's essential that Creole and Cajun should remain the default cooking styles in New Orleans, and that the leading chefs of the city should emphasize the local ingredients and cooking methods.

Here's why. The genius of New Orleans cooking is not that we cook better than anyone else. It's that nobody else in the world cooks our local specialties—except when they consciously imitate us (usually badly, I've found). The day that our food fails to be flagrantly distinctive—stops being something unique to this place—is the day we become Anywhere, USA.

That's also the day I'm leaving town.

But in the first years of the new century, hardly a chef in town was creating new Cajun or Creole dishes. The most exciting new dish with an unambiguous local flavor was Drago's charbroiled oysters, a dish so simple it's amazing nobody had served it before. Freshly shucked Louisiana oysters in their shells, topped with peppery garlic butter and Parmesan cheese, are grilled over a very hot open fire. The dish quickly turned a struggling old seafood restaurant into one of the most popular places in town. Soon everybody with oyster shells and a grill was making it. You love to see something like that.

Meanwhile, the top chefs of the city were serving braised pork belly. I remember the first person to call me about that. "I ordered this pork thing that sounded good, but it turned out to be a huge block of fat with a few streaks of lean in it, just sitting there!" the caller said, with some amazement. "Am I missing something?" What he had missed were the articles in food magazines saying that braised pork belly was in vogue. Or the reviews in New York and elsewhere adding stars to restaurants on the basis of their pork belly futures.

If I remember correctly, the first restaurant to serve braised pork belly in New Orleans was Herbsaint, an otherwise fine bistro run by

Donald Link. He was a protégé of Susan Spicer at Bayona. Susan owns a piece of the restaurant, but she lets Link's taste preside. To good effect. Herbsaint has, among other delicious things, the best frog legs served in New Orleans since the demise of LeRuth's.

It apparently was a French thing, this pork belly. Uncured, unsmoked bacon, basically. Not a lot more to it than that, cooked low and slow in a flavored stock. Oh, one more thing: It was Kurobuta pork belly. Kurobuta is to pork what Kobe is to beef. Still not enough to make it good.

A dish like that would never have gotten off the ground if someone somewhere hadn't made it well at some time. I got a clue on that when chef Patrick Perie called me one day to say he'd cooked up a batch of tripe for himself and Gerard Crozier. And me, too, if I was interested. The Lyon-born Crozier, who operated the best French bistro in New Orleans history for twenty-five years, had a French-accented prime steakhouse at the time. Perie was his chef de cuisine. Nobody cooks tripe better than a classically trained French chef, and here it was. Perfect, right enough, with a gelatin-rich sauce and—wait!—chunks of braised pork belly. Now that really was something.

After Herbsaint introduced it, braised pork belly spread like the flu from one hip menu to another across New Orleans. Diners who mentioned it on the radio or on my Web message board were all but unanimous in their opinion of it, though. They remained along the lines of that puzzled caller: "What am I missing here?" I have met people who like braised pork belly, and, as mentioned, I've had a couple of good versions myself. But whenever I see it, I think about how many more interesting Creole dishes had to die to allow that one to live, just because an aggressive meat salesperson with a folder full of reviews from thousands of miles away persuaded chefs that they had to serve it to keep up.

ASIA OPENS MORE BRANCHES

New Orleans, like other cities with a strong regional cuisine, has historically not been a fertile place for exotic cuisines to take root. But as the century turned, a new force was at work: The children of the baby boomers were beginning to come of age.

Although we baby boomers have on the whole been very lucky in the way our children are growing up, how they will manage the world when they are in charge gives me cause for concern. Of course, they're selfish, spoiled brats, just as every generation before them has been. That's not what bothers me.

What bothers me is that they have not developed a taste for Creole and Cajun cooking. Neither of my two children, for example, has ever touched red beans and rice, crawfish étouffée, bread pudding, or coffee and chicory with hot milk. No oysters (although they do like Drago's charbroiled bivalves). No shrimp, neither rémoulade nor barbecue. No grits. No muffulettas. No (heaven help us!) roast beef poor boys! Jude likes gumbo a lot; Mary Leigh doesn't.

These eating habits—or the absence thereof—seem to be common among my progeny's generation, and even the one before it. So what are they eating? The usual junk that young people eat (including me, when I was young). Burgers and pizza and all that. But as they become sophisticated, they turn not to the local seafood and gumbo house, but to the sushi bar. The Vietnamese pho shop. The Lebanese shawarma and kebab café.

That outreaching appetite finally broke down the gates for ethnic restaurateurs in New Orleans. The number of ethnic restaurants in town doubled in the ten years before Hurricane Katrina. Many of the new places, far from the minimal Chinese and Middle Eastern cafés of years ago, are very substantial, handsome restaurants. Most of them are very busy.

The new spots have certainly enriched the eating possibilities around New Orleans, and that is cause for celebration. But when I hear people talk about eating sushi twice a week; pho three times; Chinese on Sunday night; and Lebanese, Mexican, and Spanish in rotation the rest of the time, I have to ask, "How often do you eat seafood platters and red beans?"

The answers are, "When I'm at my mom's," "At the Jazz Festival," or "When friends want to go to a restaurant that serves that stuff." In other words, "Almost never."

The fate of Creole cream cheese demonstrates where this attitude leads. My mother, like many Orleanians of her generation, ate Creole cream cheese for breakfast. It's an odd item: clabbered milk, basically, lumps of curd in a juicy whey. You eat it with sugar, cream, and fruit. Every supermarket in town sold lots of it. Even the little convenience store where I worked in my teens sold ten or so boxes of Creole cream cheese every day. Then, in the late 1970s, Creole cream cheese became hard to find. In the 1980s, it almost disappeared. Around that time I had a man from Borden's—the last dairy to make the stuff for a long time—on the radio show. I asked why they had dropped the product.

"The truth is that it sells very little," he said. "If we sold a lot of it, we'd make it forever. But it's not enough to make any sense at all."

"I don't believe it," I said, and told him of the number of people who called me looking for it.

"Do you eat Creole cream cheese, Tom?"

"No," I had to say. "I never did."

"That's the problem. Your generation didn't pick up that habit. The people who like Creole cream cheese are either dead or dying."

Creole cream cheese returned when a couple of small dairies started making it as an artisanal product, for about three times the price it used to cost. Emeril gave it a boost when he started making cheesecakes with it—a great idea, taking advantage of the natural tanginess. But it's still not flying off the shelves.

Creole cream cheese aside, our salvation from this perdition was sleazy chic. The neighborhood restaurants kept coming, at an increasing pace. Some of them even had would-be celebrity chefs. By 2001, it was clear that the New Orleans neighborhood restaurant would not become extinct. In fact, there seemed to be more of the joints around than anyone under fifty could remember there ever being. Nobody could honestly explain their eating at Subway by saying they couldn't find a poor boy stand. Poor boys were everywhere.

The baby boomers and their forebears are still eating New Orleans food avidly. But if the teens and twenty-somethings drop the ball, I worry that the day will come when red beans and rice becomes as hard to find as grillades and grits, calas, Creole cream cheese, and other hits from past generations.

And that's where we were when the wind started to blow.

Windsor Court Salad

This is the best house salad being served in New Orleans. Presented beautifully, with multicolor layers in a glass bowl, it is something like the classic Cobb salad, but without the chicken. My wife Mary Ann and I had this salad on our wedding night, which we spent at the Windsor Court before heading out on our honeymoon.

Dressing

1 egg yolk
1 tsp. Dijon mustard
1 cup vegetable oil
⅓ cup red wine vinegar
1 French shallot, chopped
2 Tbs. bottled chili sauce (nearby the ketchup at the market)
Salt and pepper to taste

Salad

1 head romaine lettuce
2 bunches watercress
2 hard-boiled eggs (whites and yolks separated)
6 radishes
2 oz. Roquefort cheese
2 large tomatoes
4 slices crisp bacon
1 large ripe avocado

1. To make the dressing, beat together the egg yolk and Dijon mustard. Beating quickly, alternately add the oil and the vinegar in a steady stream to form an emulsion. Season with chopped shallots, chili sauce, and salt and pepper.

2. Chop all the salad ingredients separately. (Do not use a food processor for the lettuce, as it bruises the greens and gives it a funny taste.) Put each ingredient in a vertical layer in a glass bowl. It's colorful and dramatic, so show the finished salad to your guests before tossing with the dressing.

SERVES SIX.

PART THREE

The Big Blow

The front entrance of Antoine's. This is the part of the building that partially collapsed into the street during the hurricane.

CHAPTER NINE

Eight Hundred and Nine to Zero

A DEEP LOW

In the early afternoon on Monday, August 29, 2005, a rotating cylinder of air about thirty degrees cooler than the air around it fell into the French Quarter at about eighty miles per hour. The pressure inside this twisting air pocket was a few inches of mercury lower than the air inside the buildings below. It landed atop the 1790s mansion that, since 1868, housed the main dining room of Antoine's Restaurant.

That event wasn't witnessed by anyone or noted by instruments. It's just the best explanation anyone can come up with for what happened next. At that moment, Hurricane Katrina's extraordinarily large eye was performing its own low-pressure twist as it ran over the easternmost extremity of New Orleans. Winds well in excess of a hundred miles per hour blew through the entire city, throwing all kinds of projectiles around and ripping structures up and down.

Wind alone couldn't have blown the brick wall of Antoine's attic into the street. Not even the random gusts—some of which may have reached 150 miles per hour—would have sucked the walls of the main dining room outward until they bulged. Couldn't have yanked out the supports for the second floor, letting the first-floor ceiling sag by a couple of feet. "It was as if a bomb had gone off inside the dining room," Michael Guste told me. He's one of Antoine Alciatoire's great-great-grandsons and was the general manager of Antoine's at the time.

Many buildings as old as that one remain in the French Quarter. None sustained damage anything like it. Nor did the several other buildings in Antoine's enormous complex suffer much. A column of low-pressure air—a near-tornado spun off Katrina's eye—is the only logical explanation.

That demolition was one of Katrina's smaller acts. Its most powerful muscle was a megawave of Gulf of Mexico water at least thirty feet high, a hundred miles front to back, and three hundred miles long. When the storm pulled that onto the shore, it washed over everything with tsunami force. The 150 miles of Mississippi Gulf Coast just east of New Orleans got the worst of it. Almost nothing remained standing there except live oak trees, whose family had seen this sort of thing more than a few times and had evolved the ability to stand up to it.

In New Orleans, the storm surge pushed eleven vertical feet of extra water into Lake Pontchartrain—the tidal lake that separates New Orleans's low-lying river-silt land from the North American continent. As the hurricane passed, its winds blew south, piling the water even higher against the levees at the lakeshore. The water flowed backward through the city's drainage canals. Those canals reach three miles deep into the heart of the city, into places where the land is ten feet below sea level.

The levees on those canals could not hold a persistent stack of water twenty-plus-feet high. They broke in several places. The water poured unstoppably onto the land, fanning away from the breaks. By the end of the first day, more than 80 percent of New Orleans's East Bank land area was submerged in a flood measurable in feet.

The levee breaks could not be repaired for days. The city's drainage pumps—one of which is the world's largest—were also hors de combat. Only they could remove the water, but it would be long after the levee breaks were stopped before the pumps began running again. Floodwater stood for three weeks in some areas. The flood—not the wind—was what caused most of Katrina's devastation in New Orleans.

Meanwhile, the city descended into chaos, with local, state, and federal agencies unable to discover just how bad the disaster was. Let alone get control of it. One could only get around by helicopter or boat.

That's the short story of Hurricane Katrina in New Orleans, the worst natural disaster in the history of the United States. As the many books that tell the long story all note, most people living in New Orleans knew something like this would happen someday. Only a year before, a five-part series in *The Times-Picayune* newspaper predicted with eerie accuracy how a storm like Katrina would devastate the city.

Like most New Orleanians, my family and I were almost (but not quite!) out of harm's way when that low-pressure air pocket blew Antoine's walls out. We followed the official evacuation order given by city and state authorities. When we left, however, I had no inkling that I would be gone from my hometown longer than ever before in my life. Or how my fluffy job as a food writer would contribute to the fearsome patching job that needed to be done when I got back.

THE END

The Friday two days before that sucking air fell on Antoine's was the last day of service for most New Orleans restaurants for a long time. For all time, in some cases. On that Friday, according to my data, 809 restaurants were open in the metropolitan area. That number included all restaurants that cook and serve on premises, all the way down to neighborhood poor boy shops. I didn't count fast-food joints, supermarket delis, take-out-only operations, or other food services insignificant to the local culinary culture.

By Sunday, the number of restaurants open in the metropolitan area was zero. The city and parish officials in the area had declared the mandatory evacuation of well over a million people. Having learned a lesson in 1998's Hurricane Georges—which barely missed New Orleans but did a lot of damage anyway—officials had a reasonably good plan for directing traffic out of town. It was about the only thing that went right.

On Saturday, Mary Ann's niece Jennifer Donner called me from her home in Atlanta. "I don't know what you're planning," she said, "but if you need a place to go, you're welcome here." I told her there was little chance that Mary Ann would go along with a family evacuation, based on what had happened (nothing) during Hurricane Georges.

At midnight, I began a four-hour anchor shift on WWL Radio. The company that owns it bought WSMB in 1992, getting me and *The Food Show* in the bargain. During emergencies, they needed all the on-air personnel they had to keep information flowing. I have equipment that allows me to broadcast from my home, and access to as much information as they have in the studio. I had hosted a few hurricane all-nighters in the past, and there I was again.

WWL is one of the country's most powerful stations, blanketing the entire southeastern United States with its signal at night. It's the official source of emergency news for the area—the one that road signs tell you to tune in to during a disaster. People already on the road—and those who soon would be—were our main audience. But people were listening all over the eastern half of the country. That's where many of the calls came from, with sympathy and good-luck wishes.

The satellite images I watched and the Hurricane Center experts I spoke to through the night brought forth superlatives in my words. This was like no other hurricane I'd seen—and I'm a weather geek who's always on top of this stuff. Katrina was not only powerful but enormous, filling nearly the entire Gulf of Mexico. It was heading right for New Orleans, with nothing to weaken it or turn it away.

Throughout my four hours, I repeated a single insistent message to the listeners: Get out of town. As soon as I was off the air, I awakened Mary Ann. Although our North Shore home wasn't under evacuation orders, there was no question in my mind that we should hit the road. When I showed Mary Ann the satellite imagery, she had to agree.

We nailed plywood over the windows, packed a few days' clothes, and left for Atlanta. We weren't frightened, but my heart was heavy. That this would disrupt our lives was a given. But what form that disruption would take was the disturbing mystery. The kids, on the other hand, were thinking in terms of escaping school and having fun in Atlanta. "We are not on vacation," I kept insisting, until they were sick of hearing it. "We are refugees!"

Refugees? Compared with the thousands of New Orleanians we would see on television during the next few days, we *were* on vacation. We were in a good car, ran into only minor traffic delays, and had a place to go where we would be comfortable and welcome to stay as long as we needed to. That good luck was something hundreds of thousands of our fellow citizens dearly wished they had.

We arrived in Atlanta late Sunday evening and went right to bed. I had my broadcast rig with me, but the WWL guys said they didn't need me. It's a good thing I didn't know that I'd already hosted my last radio show for three months. It would have freaked me out.

Monday morning, Hurricane Katrina made landfall in Louisiana. We watched it all day on television. The conditions were so bad that little information was getting out to the rest of the world. But even from our safe haven we could tell how big the storm was. Five hundred miles from New Orleans, tornadoes spun off by Hurricane Katrina were setting off alarms all around Atlanta. How far did we have to go to get away from this thing?

"If you want a drink, I have martini stuff under the kitchen sink," Jennifer told me. "I keep it there for my father-in-law, but he only comes once a year. Take all you want!"

I found the bottles of Beefeater gin and Noilly Prat vermouth, poured a martini on the rocks, and sat down again. Almost as soon as I had landed, I heard the worst possible news: "We have reports of a levee breach in the Lakeview section of New Orleans," said the CNN reporter. A fist of ice settled below my sternum. Having written a number of articles about the New Orleans drainage system—a subject I find fascinating—I knew this meant major disaster. Perhaps the end of New Orleans as we knew it. To say nothing of the end of my career as I knew that.

Many martinis and many hours later, Mary Ann tapped me on the shoulder. "Come to bed," she said. "You've been watching this for fourteen hours straight."

My jaw gaped just as long the next day. Now the news media had people in New Orleans sending reports via satellite phone. Anderson Cooper had a particularly disturbing dispatch from the corner of Tchoupitoulas and Poydras, across the street from Mother's. "No one is in control here," Cooper said. "Behind me on my left, you see uniformed police officers firing at the men on my right, who are firing back. It's like the Wild West, complete with a burning building in the background!" That building . . . hmmm . . . was it Restaurant

August? The best restaurant in town was somewhere near there, anyway. I was still watching my beat.

Another martini. More levee breaks. More flooding. More chaos. People trapped on overpasses surrounded by miles of water four feet deep and more. People in New Orleans East, on the verge of drowning in their attics as the flood rose, cutting holes in their roofs to get out so they could be picked up by helicopters. Unbelievable.

Thousands were trapped with no food or water in the Superdome and the Convention Center. Looters were everywhere, stealing everything. Buildings were on fire all over the place and had to just burn themselves out, because floodwater made them inaccessible. Appalling.

No power and no communications. Police deserting their posts. The clueless Michael Brown, director of the Federal Emergency Management Agency (FEMA, an acronym that lives in infamy for most Orleanians, as well as in the name of a sushi roll served all over town after the storm), saying absurd things. Another martini. Another. I was not a martini drinker until then. I am now.

Each day, the news was worse than the day before. No matter where New Orleanians were—in the squalid Superdome with the hole in its roof, or safely ensconced in a friendly remove hundreds of miles away—they saw the lives they knew evaporating. What would we all do now?

Many of us had the same curious feeling in those moments. Instead of an oppressive weight loaded upon us, many of us felt unshackled from the responsibilities of our pre-Katrina lives. I heard that from many friends during our ceaseless debriefings with one another after the storm.

Mary Ann was surprised to hear that I felt that way. I was in her opinion an incorrigible New Orleans lifer. But she had long wanted to leave New Orleans, and she saw Katrina as a likely chance. If she could talk me into it. I was weightless for only a few days, though. I soon started thinking about what I'd do when I went back. On the other hand, Mary Ann and the kids never lost their feelings of freedom from New Orleans.

This same dichotomy affected nearly every New Orleans family, striking at the heart of the community.

The Bottom

New Orleans remained officially evacuated for weeks. It seemed the city couldn't catch a break. Just as a few people began to return, about four weeks after Katrina, a second storm—Rita, which in some ways was even more powerful than Katrina—forced a reevacuation of New Orleans and a reflooding of some areas. That delayed the mass return of citizens until October.

Throughout this time the authorities were still trying to force diehards out, and they continued to prevent anyone from returning. Residents who refused to budge sometimes did so while holding a rifle. A particularly adamant bunch hung on in the French Quarter, little of which was flooded. Right on the river, it's on the highest land in town. That's why Bienville landed there. Enough Quarterites remained that Johnny White's Bar on Bourbon Street—a place that was at best only half sleazy chic—never did close, the authorities be damned. They served a little food, too, so it could be said (although I won't) that the count of restaurants went not from 809 to zip, but to 1.

One of those who stayed on was Dr. Brobson Lutz, the former New Orleans health director. A gourmet, bon vivant, regular caller to my radio show, and longtime French Quarter resident, he rode out the hurricane in his apartment—next door to the one Tennessee Williams lived in for many years. He was forced to depart only when the city cut off water service to the French Quarter. "That's how they finally got us to leave," he told me. "We were concerned about fire." As for the water itself, he said that at no time was the municipal water supply unsafe in the French Quarter, or in most of the rest of the city, for that matter. He came back five days later, when the water came back on.

Brobson sent many dispatches to me by e-mail. I learned from him that some of the finest French Quarter restaurants held magnificent feeds during the day or two after the storm passed. They had coolers full of food that would soon be garbage, so they cooked it all and gave it to their fellow holdouts. Galatoire's and Antoine's had two of the best such banquets, hauling out whole beef tenderloins and beautiful fish, grilling it (no sauces under this duress), and passing it out to a grubbier bunch of people than they'd served in a long time.

Many of those were, however, the same people they usually served. That was the end of serious eating for more than a little while.

The French Quarter was exceptional in not being flooded. That saving grace extended all along the river, whose banks are the high ground in this reclaimed marshland. The Central Business District and Uptown areas also harbored people who refused to leave, people who either kept a lid on things or looted. The police, even with the help of the Army and the National Guard, couldn't do it all.

Helping the Army and the National Guard through the worst days became a strategy for being allowed to stay. That's what chef Horst Pfeifer did. He was the owner of Bella Luna, a beautiful restaurant on the riverfront that was too badly damaged by Katrina ever to reopen. But he also had a large catering facility a block away from the Convention Center, where one of the worst crises unfolded in the days after the storm. Horst was there throughout the storm and after. He told me that he'd struck a deal with the troops: He'd cook for them if they would keep him supplied with electricity and water. He used all the food he had, and the troops made it easy for him to get more. Horst was always terrific, but during the week after Katrina he was without question the best chef working in New Orleans.

Outside the strip of dry ground along the river, though, the city was deserted. Only the dead and a few of the stranded remained in the three-fourths of the city's former land area where the water was high. It sounds macabre, but it was true. The people of New Orleans were (as the local saying goes, rhyming the two words) "gone pecan." No people, no city. *The Times-Picayune*'s huge headline on September 1 was no exaggeration: "**hitting bottom.**"

It took two weeks for New Orleans to begin its painfully slow rise from absolute zero. During that time, all that most people could do was watch on television how bad things continued to be. Even if you could go back to town—and the authorities said you couldn't—where would you go? What would you do?

Finally, enough drainage pumps were brought back to life that the floodwater began receding from the bowl-shaped terrain. (Water can't leave New Orleans by gravity; it has to be pumped out.)

Making phone contact with anyone in New Orleans remained difficult for weeks. But enough information about the state of eating filtered out by e-mail and text message that I resumed publishing *The New Orleans Menu Daily* nearly every day, beginning the day after the storm.

The earliest reports from my correspondents, as they scrambled to find something to eat, had to do with the military MREs (meals ready to eat). These and hundreds of thousands of bottles of water arrived in a parade of military vehicles to the Superdome, where many people were still trapped. The MREs made their way—often by boat, the only way to get to many areas—to people trapped without resources. They were allowed whole cases of them, with enough variety that the eaters began discussing which were the best. This later became an ongoing topic on my radio show. While I heard good things about the barbecue meatballs, I'm glad I missed that part of the recovery menu.

Next, reports started arriving from Metairie. That's the biggest New Orleans suburb, just west of the city, in Jefferson Parish. It also had flooding, but not on the scale that New Orleans experienced. Its drainage system was configured differently than the century-old pumping stations and canals in New Orleans, so most of the floodwater was pumped out in a matter of days instead of weeks. It was also ten miles farther from the eye's path. Although power was still out, people returned home to stay after about ten days. When they did, they found very few businesses with food and supplies open. But among those few that were, incredibly, were some restaurants. Several Metairie eateries claim to have been the first to open after the storm, and I don't know who to believe. At that stage, the health inspections that would later be required for reopening restaurants hadn't begun, so there's no telling.

But there's no doubt that Drago's was one of the very first. Nor that its opening was the most heroic. Its Croatian-immigrant owners had already distinguished themselves by organizing a massive relief effort during the war in Bosnia. The supplies filled their bar for weeks. When Drago, Klara, and Tommy Cvitanovich came back to town, before they even addressed the little matter of the flooding of and damage to their homes, they opened Drago's restaurant to hungry people. They began cooking and serving free meals to anyone who came by—many of whom really were in serious distress.

Drago's kept that program going for two months, while slowly evolving back into a regular restaurant. It ultimately served 77,000 free meals—an amazing effort for a family-owned, one-location restaurant. The owners viewed it as something they had to do from a purely moral perspective.

Chef Paul Prudhomme also swung into action to get people fed. Right after the evacuation orders were lifted, he showed up at the Metairie plant that produces his spices and other retail products. He set up a kitchen and cooked for anyone who needed to eat, for free. That went on until he was able to get into K-Paul's in the French Quarter, more than a month later.

At first, it was everything the returning people of Metairie could do just to get enough food to live on. It wasn't long, however, before there were enough people to reopen more stores and restaurants. And that's when I first heard of an unexpected, encouraging trend: Any restaurant that managed to get its doors open was besieged. Not by people who were starving to death, but by customers who were looking for any way to reconnect with their former lives. Real food from a real restaurant performed that magic better than almost anything else could. They would wait hours to get it.

The restaurateurs, eager to get back to work and seeing the demand, opened as fast as they could. Some Metairie places began service during their reconstructions. People filled tables in formerly fancy dining rooms that now had exposed studs and bare concrete floors, sometimes illuminated only by the light coming through the windows.

The customers were blinded to these deficiencies by the glowing promise of real food. They returned to their favorite restaurants— and also those they'd never heard of—as soon as they could. The restaurants were mobbed with eager diners. Ed McIntyre, who owned two Metairie restaurants, told me that one of them was grossing $2 million a month for the first few months after the hurricane. On an annual basis, that would have made it the highest-volume restaurant in town before the storm.

An Old Home and a New Home

The part of the North Shore where we lived had its own brand of damage, mostly having to do with fallen pine trees landing atop houses and power lines. But it was an order of magnitude less severe than the travails of the other side of the lake.

On the ninth day after the hurricane, Mary Ann and I drove home to look things over and check on relatives. Our home was undamaged. But almost all the power poles and lines throughout the area were on the ground, knocked down by the now-horizontal pines. The tangle was formidable.

Like everybody else in the storm-hit area, we had a particularly disgusting mess to clean up. With the power out so long, and with the heat wave that followed the hurricane, everything in everybody's refrigerators and freezers had gone very sour. I discovered that chicken stored at ninety degrees becomes a liquid after nine days. And other gross food-spoilage facts. We threw everything into the woods that surround our home.

The cleanup was less convenient for people in the city, who had neither woods nor garbage pickups. They were told to dig holes in their lawns and to bury the contents of their refrigerators in them. Vivid stories about refrigerators gone bad were a rare source of comic relief. A briskly selling book that came out later was a collection of photos of abandoned refrigerators and the spray-painted warnings about the evils lurking inside them.

Chefs told me stories about their much larger piles of fermenting foodstuffs. The consensus was that nothing was more revolting to deal with than oysters off refrigeration for a month.

The water in our home comes from an electric pump on a well. It was obvious to us upon our return that we wouldn't have power for a very long time. But while you can live without electricity, you can't live without water. That cinched our plans. We cleaned up the worst messes, and ourselves, until the water in the tank ran out. Then we spent a sweltering, pitch-black, spooky night trying to sleep. The chorus of animals outside was loud—and sounded happy. What does a frog or a katydid care about a hurricane?

We returned to Atlanta in two cars. (We were so sure that we'd be right back when we evacuated that we'd left one behind.) The solo 500-mile trip gave me a lot of time to think. Our future was up in the air. The radio station still had me on payroll, but how long could that last? I still wrote and published *The New Orleans Menu* on my own Web site, but would NewOrleans.com—which paid me for publishing my words—return? Would being a food writer be a viable career in New Orleans at all anymore?

On the other hand, I had something to keep me busy. Before the storm, I was about finished writing and testing the recipes for a cookbook I planned on publishing myself. The strange feeling of freedom that came over me during the evacuation, however, emboldened me to seek a publisher. And I got one: Stewart, Tabori & Chang, whose cookbooks I'd long admired. They were eager not only to take the book but to rush its publication. I was so thankful that I decided to give half the royalties to Habitat for Humanity, to contribute something to the rebuilding of my city.

Though it seemed counterintuitive, somehow I had the feeling that our food culture would become a critical machine to stitch us back together. And if that were true, morally I had to be involved. Besides, good luck continued to remain with me and my family, to an almost embarrassing degree. Many close friends became homeless, or otherwise saw their lives rendered unrecognizable. I knew quite a few people who died as a direct or indirect result of the storm. The worst of our problems would fall into the category of inconvenience.

Mary Ann's sister Christine Thron lives in the Washington, DC, area. She thought we should go there to ride out the long-term evacuation. She had even contacted schools, which eagerly offered to accept Jude and Mary Leigh in their classrooms, no questions asked. This was the beginning of an outpouring of assistance that we found everywhere we went. The people of America were sympathetic and generous to New Orleanians wherever they showed up.

They were, that is, unless too many supplicants hit them at one time. The television coverage of the hospitality offered by Houston to the thousands of newly homeless New Orleanians filled us with gratitude. But it was obvious that it was a strain both for the hosts and the guests, because of the sheer number of people who needed help. In Washington, however, we competed with few other evacuees for the lavish generosity.

So I learned some new advice to share with my listeners next time I had to get them though the night before a hurricane. First rule: Leave at midnight, and you won't get caught in miles of traffic. Second rule: Evacuate to as distant a point as you possibly can.

PART FOUR

Food Saves
New Orleans

The ancient bag label from Union Coffee and Chicory, the old-style brew I drink every morning.

CHAPTER TEN

Rebirth Begins in the Kitchen

CRAZY LANDSCAPE

New Orleans came out of its coma in the final week of September 2005, about a month after the storm. As soon as Hurricane Rita turned west, and the high tides from it subsided, the pumping out of the city resumed. New Orleans citizens were allowed to return, one neighborhood at a time.

We thought the heavy coverage of the Katrina aftermath on television had prepared us for the worst. As it turned out, it wasn't the extent of the destruction that got to us, but the nature of it. *Nature* is the perfect word here. Nature displayed a repertoire of tricks that it doesn't use very often, and that most of us had never seen. The mess wasn't just heartbreaking, but bizarre. Certain sights, seen everywhere throughout the flood zone, were like nothing in anyone's prior experience. Hairlike mold growing six inches high from carpets and wallboard, for example.

The visual that lingers in my mind (and those of most others) was the combination of two marks on the walls of buildings. We'd never seen them before, and we hope we never will again. The first mark was a greasy brown, perfectly straight horizontal line that went all the way around everything, standing more than a few feet high. It showed the level at which the flood settled. Some buildings had two or more of these stripes, recording the punctuated progress in the draining of the city. It took me two years (equal to the time it took for the marks to wash off) to stop checking out the flood lines as I traveled around town.

The second mark was more lurid. An X in fluorescent orange

spray paint emblazoned the front of every edifice in the flood zones, usually right next to the entrance. In each quadrant of the X was a code, identifying which emergency crew had been inside the building, the date, what had been found, and, finally, miscellaneous information. That last quadrant sometimes mentioned pets left behind, many of them still alive. But sometimes it reported something much worse. The title of the most celebrated book about Katrina, by *Times-Picayune* columnist Chris Rose, quotes from that latter kind: *1 Dead in Attic.*

The storm was ignorant of race or income. An equal-opportunity destroyer. The Lower Ninth Ward, a historic, lower-middle-class (although Fats Domino lived there), mostly black neighborhood, caught flood tides from two different directions. It was devastated so thoroughly in its northern half that hardly a structure remained standing. But just over the parish line, in mostly white, middle-class St. Bernard Parish, the damage was every bit as bad—with the added aggravation of an oil spill from a gasoline refinery. Metairie Club Gardens, one of the two or three most affluent sections in the New Orleans area, was the only part of Metairie that got the over-your-head, weeks-long flooding that Orleans Parish did.

Deep flooding affected everyone in between. The first house Mary Ann and I lived in together, in the pleasant old Mid-City section, had nine feet of water climbing its walls. The 1880s house next door was so weakened that it toppled over onto our former home.

Of course, it was harder for low-income homeowners and renters to come back than it was for those with more substantial resources, even when they suffered comparable damage. I lost the producer of my radio show that way. The expense of rebuilding his badly flooded house in New Orleans East made no economic sense to him. He just abandoned the place and relocated permanently to where he had evacuated, in Houston.

That effect would prove to be the most daunting obstacle to the return of the New Orleans restaurant community. While the customers who were able to return to town and attempt to rebuild were jamming the restaurants with people, restaurant employees—whose incomes tended to be at the lower end of the scale—were nowhere to be found.

The most curious staff diaspora afflicted Antoine's. The old restaurant has a history of dynastic employees. Many of the waiters, cooks, and even dishwashers are children, grandchildren, and nieces and nephews of other Antoine's hands, sometimes going back several generations. Because of that, a wildly disproportionate number of Antoine's people came from the same parts of town: the Ninth Ward in New Orleans proper and the Chalmette and Arabi suburbs in St. Bernard Parish. Katrina dealt those areas its worst depredations, leaving hardly a single habitable house. The extended families of people in those places have a way of also living there. The displaced couldn't stay with their aunts and uncles, because the aunts and uncles lived three blocks away and experienced exactly the same problems.

For a time, Antoine's leased space on a ship moored at a wharf—and not a cruise ship, either. Many of its employees slept in bunks for months while trying to figure out what to do next. It says something about the importance of the restaurant that few of them so much as considered leaving Antoine's employ.

And neither they nor the management were sure Antoine's would survive. The repair of its main building—the one the column of low-pressure air sucked outward and downward—was very complicated and expensive. In an early interview in the *Chicago Tribune*, the restaurant's owners hinted at the chilling prospect that the restaurant's 165-year history was over. If an essential culinary landmark like Antoine's disappeared, how much more of the New Orleans restaurant community would go, too?

Twenty-two Restaurants

Fortunately, the undamaged restaurants (there weren't many) thought the risk was worth taking and got the ball rolling. The first restaurants to reopen in New Orleans proper were in the French Quarter and along the Uptown riverfront. Magazine Street—which follows the crescent of the river and is close enough to it that it was well above the flood line—became the post-Katrina restaurant row.

The earliest returning New Orleans eateries encountered the same urgency among their customers that their counterparts in Metairie did. But the surrounding environment was very different. While the suburbs were bustling with people streaming in to return to and repair their homes and businesses, a deathly quiet reigned over most of New Orleans itself. Vincent Catalanotto, whose Uptown Italian restaurant opened less than two weeks after Katrina, told me things were spooky. "We were going crazy serving people inside," he said. "But if you walked outside, you knew something was really wrong. No cars on the street, parked or moving. No people."

It was around that time that I made up my first list of open restaurants and published it on NOMenu.com. It showed twenty-two restaurants open in the entire metropolitan area. Most of them were in Metairie or on the North Shore. By the end of September, I was adding two or three new reopenings to the tally every day, with the greatest growth in the French Quarter and Uptown.

Dr. Brobson Lutz, still adamant about remaining in his French Quarter apartment, was one of a number of people on the ground who kept me up-to-date until I was back in town. He was particularly excited about a brand-new restaurant named Stanley. "The first really functioning restaurant (menu, take all comers, martinis with olives, air-conditioned) has opened in New Orleans," he wrote me on September 15, 2005, two and a half weeks after the hurricane. "Scott Boswell's Stanley is on Decatur Street. He's running off a generator, cooking on a charcoal grill in the courtyard of his old restaurant." Boswell's main place, which would not reopen for over a year, was Stella! It was and is one of the two or three best restaurants in New Orleans.

Two especially significant returnees were Ralph Brennan's French Quarter restaurants. The Red Fish Grill fired itself back up on September 29, and his Italian trattoria Bacco opened the very next day. Ralph and his staff were the first to develop a strategy to make sure their food would be safe to eat. They used disposable everything, boiled tap water (still declared off-limits for drinking by the city) for clean-up purposes, and bottled water for all cooking and drinking.

At the time, the Louisiana Department of Health and Hospitals, which licenses and inspects restaurants, hadn't worked out the details of how to recertify them. Perhaps because of the eminence of the Brennans, the agency studied what Ralph had done in his places. From that they developed the criteria that had to be met before restaurants could resume service. Establishments passing the new inspections got pink cards to post in their windows. Those joined the flood-level strips and the orange Xs as icons of the post-storm months. Although they're now obsolete, many restaurants still have their pink cards on display, as if bragging that they were there in the really bad days and survived them.

Ralph was the luckiest of the Brennans, and perhaps the most fortunate local restaurateur of all. Neither of his French Quarter places sustained significant damage. He had a third restaurant, Ralph's on the Park, in the center of the city; it was surrounded by some of the deepest and nastiest floodwaters. But when Ralph finally got over there, he was stunned to see that the only damage to his place was a single small broken window. The restaurant, built in 1869, was on the Metairie Ridge, the banks of the Mississippi River tens of thousands of years ago. Not a trickle of the flood made it inside Ralph's on the Park. And no looters swam through the water to get there.

The Toll

As encouraging as those signs were, the flow of depressing news seemed to be picking up speed. In addition to the estimated one thousand people who had lost their lives as a direct result of the storm, the obituary pages reported many more deaths than usual of people who had escaped the physical power of the storm, but not its mental and spiritual repercussions. The end of the world as they knew it stole the will to live from many, many New Orleanians.

The death of good old Cliff Lachney was the first to bring tears to my eyes. He was the maître d' at Antoine's long before I first dined there in 1969. He was still there, at seventy-one, when Katrina hit. For me and most other customers, Cliff was the face of Antoine's. He opened the door for you and ushered you to your table, apologizing all the way for anything you might perceive as even slightly imperfect. Between lunch and dinner, he'd stroll over to the Cabildo and play country songs on his guitar for tips. Now and then, always unannounced (I encouraged him to do this), he'd show up on the radio show and play a song or two and talk about the restaurant and its customers. Cliff tried to ride out the storm with his son, who had a mental handicap, in their Lakeview home. It was close to the levee break, and filled with more than ten feet of water. They drowned on the second floor.

In all of New Orleans, it would have been hard to find two more beloved people than Mary and Ernest Hansen, the owners of Hansen's Sno-Bliz Shop. For seventy-plus years, using a machine Ernest had built himself, they personally ground hard-frozen blocks of ice into a powder, then doused them with the flavored syrups Mary made fresh every morning. While the idea of wetting down ground ice with a sweet liquid is widespread and ancient, nowhere in the world is it more popular or taken to greater extremes than it is in New Orleans. Sno-ball stands are everywhere, a local cultural phenomenon of such importance that non-Orleanians find it hard to believe.

At Hansen's, the undisputed ne plus ultra of sno-ball stands, Mary and Ernest did everything themselves, following standards so stringent that it took them twice as long as anyone else to make a sno-ball. That dedication created a line out on the sidewalk that equaled the one at Galatoire's on a busy day. Standing in that queue for as long as an hour while shooting the breeze (in the complete lack of breeze, and matching temperature and humidity in the nineties) with newly made friends was as much a part of Uptown New Orleans life as anything else you could name.

The Hansens always told me that my writing about them in the 1970s put Sno-Bliz on the map. That is absurd, and I told them so. But I was not allowed to stand in line for a Sno-Bliz. Ernest would grab my arm and, while calling me "cousin" for the benefit of the crowd, escort me into the backroom—the only air-conditioned spot in the place. He'd put all other orders on hold while he and Mary made me a bigger Sno-Bliz, with more stuff on and in it, than I had asked for. This is the first time I've admitted this in print. I held back for fear that other Hansen's customers would hate me for it. What could I do? Nobody told Mary Hansen how to run her shop.

The Hansens were both in their nineties when they evacuated from Katrina to their son's home in Thibodaux. Mary was quite ill at the time. She died a few days after the storm. Ernest, who compared their romance to Romeo and Juliet's, surprised no one when he passed away a few months later. The news of the Hansens' departure was a downer of heavy weight for tens of thousands of people. Fortunately, their legend lives on. Their granddaughter Ashley keeps the shop running, using the same machine and same standards Mary and Ernest upheld.

Austin Leslie, too. When Richard Collin began encouraging everyone to enter predominantly black neighborhoods in search of great Creole cooking, Austin Leslie was his favorite soul-food chef. He became everyone else's, too. Austin was the owner of Chez Helene, whose dishes are still being copied widely around town. (In 2009, a new restaurant called Austin's Creole Café opened, in homage.)

After he closed Chez Helene, Austin traveled all over the world, cooking his Creole food. He also consulted with numerous restaurants—most famously Jacques-Imo's. He was a gregarious guy who loved to cook. His ever-smiling face, topped with his ship-captain's cap, was immediately recognizable to every avid New Orleans eater. Austin was another Orleanian who tried to endure the hurricane at home. He was trapped by floodwaters in his attic for two days in near-hundred-degree heat. He died a month later in Atlanta, at seventy-one—the most regretted loss of a chef as a result of Katrina.

And then there was Harry Tervalon. Harry worked for nearly fifty years slinging hamburgers, omelets, and clever remarks at the customers of the Camellia Grill. Any poll of New Orleans eaters to reveal the greatest New Orleans waiter of all time inevitably elected Harry by a landslide. Although the other waiters at the Camellia Grill were infected by his bonhomie, there never was and never will be another Harry. He always had a funny joke to tell, and in between, as he danced around the grill cooks and the other waiters, he had a line of patter that was both familiar and incomprehensible. His answer to "How are you, Harry?" often included the phrase, "Chilly in Gentilly, two below in Tupelo." He lived his whole life in New Orleans, but he had a passion for the New York Yankees. That resounded with the Tulane University students who filled the Grill, since many of them were from the Northeast. Harry served me for thirty-five years, and we were good friends. He never seemed to change, creating the illusion that he would be behind the counter at the Camellia Grill forever.

That the hurricane could take down the irrepressible good humor of Harry Tervalon is testimony to its power. Harry's house in chilly Gentilly went deep underwater. He fixed it and moved back in anyway. But he wasn't the same, and other health problems circled around him. When he died two years after the hurricane, the obituary, written by his son, gave as the cause of death "cancer, and the failure of the federal levee system." I was not surprised to see Harry's funeral filled with the most recognizable people in New Orleans. If Harry never waited on you, your life list of New Orleans experiences is missing a big one.

I'M COMING HOME

I kept up with all these developments while still evacuated in Washington, DC. I carried on with *The New Orleans Menu Daily*, and even resumed my weekly dining column in *CityBusiness*, a spin-off of *Figaro* that I had started writing for after *Figaro* folded in 1980. I began receiving an unprecedented amount of mail from my readers, specifically encouraging me to continue my coverage of the seemingly inconsequential food scene.

I clearly needed to get back into that scene in person. But, as was true for everybody else who wanted to return, finding a place to live was a daunting prospect. And my family had no inclination to return home. The kids loved the schools that had adopted them, and the change of scenery to this much larger, wealthier city. Even though the living arrangements in Mary Ann's sister's home were suboptimal (her family really didn't have the space, even though they insisted that it was OK), my family preferred sleeping on the floor in Maryland to what they saw happening in New Orleans.

My own living arrangements were more comfortable, but still spartan. I was holed up five miles away in the basement of Mary Ann's sister's mother-in-law's basement. "Mom-Mom" was a sweet little eighty-four-year-old woman. Her basement was very quiet. I got an immense amount of writing done there, even by my usual standard of 5,000 or so words a day. It allowed me to finish my cookbook. I had already completed all the kitchen testing and most of the recipe writing in the previous two years. It seems impossible now, but I pulled the whole 336-page work together in just a week. With the radio show and other distractions at home, it probably would have taken a year.

That done, I wrote a few freelance articles for Washington-area publications. I thought I'd better get a toehold in case it became necessary for us to stay there for keeps. In September 2005, no New Orleanian either in or out of town had any idea what the city's future might be.

The first story I sold was about the difficulty I encountered in finding coffee and chicory in Maryland. That blue-black blend, usually served with hot milk, is a must for me and many other Orleanians in the morning. But it's not easily found outside New Orleans. For the same story, I also reviewed a couple of DC restaurants that served credible New Orleans–style food. When I spoke to the chef of one of them, he told me—not knowing who I was—that he pulled most of his recipes from a New Orleans–based Web site. Turned out it was my own. No wonder I liked his food!

I also looked into DC-area radio. My status as a New Orleans evacuee always won open-arms welcomes from programmers. Nobody had a job for me, but they were all intrigued. The most interesting interview was with the program director of a major news-talk station. It went something like this:

"So, you do a talk show! What else do you talk about besides food?"

"That's it."

"What, is it a weekend show?"

"No, three hours every day, in afternoon drive time. Food and wine and cooking and restaurants."

"Come on! That's impossible. You can't do that on radio!" And they wouldn't consider letting me do it there.

A couple of days after that meeting, I had lunch with a fellow evacuee, a professor at the University of New Orleans and a reader of my newsletter. I hadn't known him before. We met at an excellent downtown Italian restaurant called Galileo. We implemented the standard New Orleans Friday lunch plan: A cocktail. Another cocktail. A bottle of wine and appetizers. Entrées and . . . did we have another bottle of wine? I don't remember.

Well into our repast, I noticed the manager hovering around our table. When I asked if we were laughing too loudly or staying too long, he said, "Not at all! But you guys aren't from here, are you?"

"No," I said. "New Orleans. How did you know?"

"New Orleans! That figures. I knew because you've been here for two and a half hours, and all you've talked about is eating."

"Well, your food is worth talking about," I replied.

"We think so, thanks," he said. "But in this town, when two guys have lunch together, we could feed them anything, and they'd just keep talking about politics."

That's when I knew that, whether I went back to New Orleans or not, Washington, DC, was not the city for me.

On October 7, my neighbor Lee Caston (who remained in his New Orleans house across the pond from me during the storm, but wished he hadn't) called with astonishing news. The power was back on. How was it possible? I didn't know, but my mind reeled with thoughts of heading home. At the very least, I'd check things out for a week or two and decide what to do after that. I did, however, take all my belongings with me; I think I'd already made up my mind.

Two days later, I drove west into the Shenandoah Valley, and then southwest on a nearly straight line to New Orleans. It was a singularly peaceful, beautiful drive. I spent the night in Knoxville, and completed the trip. The entire way, an obscure Johnny Mathis song, "I'm Coming Home," played in my head. I hadn't heard it for at least thirty-five years.

The traffic on the last leg of the ride told a tale. I passed convoy after convoy of trailers en route to New Orleans. The city needed tens of thousands of them to shelter people whose homes had been destroyed. And even though I'd already seen it, I was appalled all over again by the destruction. Hattiesburg, Mississippi, more than a hundred miles inland, looked as if it had taken a direct hit. The downed trees along the road were uncountable.

Five miles from home, I pulled off the interstate and into the Winn-Dixie supermarket. The minute I walked into that familiar store, my heart leaped, and I grinned uncontrollably. Home was still right where I'd left it. I didn't see anyone I knew, but I talked to everybody in the store and in the long checkout lines. That's how it was then, and would be for months. Hurricane Katrina was the obsession. We'd talk about it for hours. But, in between storm episodes, we talked about what we'd eat once we settled back in. That, more than anything else, convinced us that we really were back home.

I bought all my favorite comfort foods: fresh oranges for juice in the morning, coffee and chicory and milk to make café au lait, White Lily self-rising flour for buttermilk biscuits. Red beans, rice, and hot sausage. No dish had been on my mind more than red beans, the traditional New Orleans lunch special. My mother made it every Monday, no matter what, when we were growing up. No dish would say "I'm home!" more convincingly than that one. I had an actual hunger for it. I have eaten more red beans and rice in the four years since Katrina than I did in the previous thirty combined.

My heart was bursting when I pulled through the gaps cut in the fallen trees and rolled over the dead power lines on the road leading to the modest rural cottage I call the Cool Water Ranch. Ecstatic. There was no chance on earth that I wouldn't be staying. And it only got better.

Café au Lait

The two cups of café au lait I have every morning are a wonderful addiction. I make them with Union coffee and chicory, brewed so dark that it leaves the side of the cup deep brown for a moment when I swirl it. I mix that with an equal amount of milk, and the pleasure commences.

I truly don't understand why everyone in the world doesn't drink coffee and chicory. The use of chicory in coffee began during a coffee shortage in the reign of Napoleon. It spread to New Orleans, where it remained the vogue after people everywhere else stopped drinking it. The chicory is the root of a variety of endive, roasted and ground. It doesn't really taste like coffee, but the flavor it adds is quite complementary. One other benefit: Chicory, while contributing about 65 percent of the brew's intensity, has no caffeine.

Serious purists insist that great coffee and chicory can only be brewed in an enamel coffee "biggin," to which you must add the hot water a little at a time, manually. I find that a good drip coffeemaker—especially the kind with cone-shaped filters—does just as fine a job, if you use enough coffee. Err on the side of too much ground coffee, and step it back if it's too strong.

Union coffee and chicory comes in a soft green bag and is a challenge to find even in New Orleans. Other good brands include CDM, French Market, and the widely distributed but relatively light Community New Orleans Blend.

½ cup ground coffee and chicory
8 cups water
6 cups milk
sugar to taste

1. Brew the coffee normally in a drip coffeemaker.
2. Fill mugs halfway full with milk, and heat in a microwave oven until steaming. Add sugar to your taste, and stir. Pour the coffee in, and observe the pleasant light foam of the milk on the coffee.

SERVES EIGHT. OR, MORE LIKELY, FOUR.

Barbecue Shrimp

Barbecue shrimp, one of the four or five best dishes in all of New Orleans cooking, is completely misnamed. The shrimp are neither grilled nor smoked, and there's no barbecue sauce. It was created in the mid-1950s at Pascal's Manale Restaurant. The dish is simple: huge whole shrimp in a tremendous amount of butter and black pepper. The essential ingredient is large, heads-on shrimp, since the fat in the shrimp heads contributes most of the flavor. Resist the urge to add lots of herbs or garlic.

Except for a revolutionary recipe Emeril came up with, barbecue shrimp is and always has been a sleazy chic dish. There's no way to eat it without getting your fingers covered with the sauce and otherwise making a mess.

3 lbs. fresh Gulf shrimp with heads on, 16–20 count to the pound
1 Tbs. lemon juice
¼ cup dry white wine
2 tsp. Worcestershire sauce
2 cloves garlic, chopped
¼ cup black pepper
2 tsp. paprika
¼ tsp. salt
3 sticks butter, softened
1 loaf French bread

1. Rinse the shrimp, and shake the excess water from them. Put them in a large skillet (or two) over medium heat, and pour the lemon juice, wine, Worcestershire, and garlic over them. Bring to a light boil, and cook, agitating the dish, until the shrimp turn pink.

2. Cover the shrimp with a thin but complete layer of black pepper. You must be bold with this. Trust me, it is almost impossible to use too much pepper in this dish. Continue to cook another couple of minutes, then sprinkle the paprika and salt over the pan.

3. Lower the heat to the minimum. Cut the butter into tablespoon-size pieces, and add three at a time to the pan, agitating the pan as the

butter melts over the shrimp. When one batch is completely melted, add another, until all the butter is used. Keep agitating the pan to make a creamy-looking, orange-hued sauce.

4. When all the butter is incorporated, serve the shrimp with lots of the sauce in bowls. Serve with hot French bread for dipping. Also plenty of napkins, and perhaps bibs.

SERVES FOUR TO SIX.

RECIPE

Red Beans and Rice

Red beans and rice is the official Monday dish in New Orleans, found on that day in restaurants of almost every kind, all over town. Although most people agree on the recipe, the trend in recent years—especially in restaurants—has been to make the sauce matrix much thicker than I remember growing up with. This version is the old (and, I think, better) style, with a looser sauce.

I have, however, added two wrinkles. One came from a radio listener, who advised that the beans improve greatly when you add much more celery than the standard recipe calls for. That proved to be correct. Also, the herb summer savory (sometimes just called savory) adds a nice flavor complement. If you can't find savory, use oregano, or just leave it out.

Red beans are classically served with smoked sausage, but they're also great with fried chicken, oysters en brochette, or grilled ham. But the ultimate is chaurice—Creole hot sausage—grilled to order and transferred, along with all the dripping fat, atop the beans.

1 lb. dried red beans
¼ lb. bacon or fatty ham
½ green bell pepper, seeded and chopped
1 small onion, chopped

3 ribs celery, chopped
12 sprigs parsley, chopped
4 cloves garlic, minced
3 qts. water
2 tsp. salt
1 bay leaf
1 tsp. savory
½ tsp. black pepper
1 tsp. Tabasco
¼ cup green onion tops, chopped
2 Tbs. parsley, chopped

1. Sort through the beans, and pick out any bad or misshapen ones. Soak the beans in cold water overnight. When ready to cook, pour off the soaking water.

2. In a large, heavy pot or Dutch oven, fry the bacon or ham fat till crisp. Remove the bacon or ham fat, and set aside for garnish (or a snack while you cook).

3. In the hot fat, sauté the bell pepper, onion, celery, parsley, and garlic until it just begins to brown. Add the beans and three quarts of water. Bring to a light boil, then lower to a simmer. Add the salt, bay leaf, savory, black pepper, and Tabasco.

4. Simmer the beans, uncovered, for two hours, stirring two or three times per hour. Add a little more water if the sauce gets too thick.

5. Mash about a half cup of the beans (more if you like them extra creamy), and stir them in into the remainder. Add salt and more Tabasco to taste. Serve the beans over rice, cooked firm. Garnish with chopped green onions and parsley.

The Ultimate: Grill some patties of Creole hot sausage and deposit them, along with as much of the fat as you can permit yourself, atop the beans. Red beans seem to have a limitless tolerance for added fat.

Meatless Alternative: Leave the pork out of the recipe

completely, and begin by sautéing the vegetables, other than the beans, in ¼ cup olive oil. At the table, pour extra-virgin olive oil over the beans. This may sound and look a bit odd, but the taste is terrific, and everything on the plate—beans, rice, and olive oil—is a proven cholesterol-lowerer.

SERVES SIX TO EIGHT.

RECIPE

Root Beer–Glazed Ham

This is the most asked-for recipe on my radio show, especially during the holidays. While baking, it makes the whole house smell good. Your guests will fight over the sweet, crusty parts of the ham. Use a lean, naturally smoked boneless ham (in New Orleans the best is Chisesi's VIP ham).

Glaze

24 oz. (2 cans) Barq's root beer
1½ Tbs. pepper jelly
1 bay leaf
1½ Tbs. Tabasco Caribbean-style steak sauce (or Pickapeppa)
6 cloves
1 stick cinnamon
Peel and juice of half an orange
Peel of half a lemon

Ham

1 cured, smoked ham, about 8 to 10 lbs.
½ tsp. dry mustard
¾ cup dark brown sugar

1. Combine all the glaze ingredients in a saucepan over medium-low heat. Bring the mixture to a simmer and cook for about a half hour. Strain and discard the solids. Reduce the liquid to about a half cup.

2. Preheat oven to 350 degrees. Place the ham on a rack in broiling pan. Cut shallow crisscross gashes across the top half. Spoon the glaze over the ham, to completely wet the surface.

3. Combine the dry mustard and the brown sugar, and pat the mixture all over the ham. Pour a half cup of water into the pan, and put the ham into the preheated oven.

4. Spoon some of the glaze over the top of the ham at fifteen-minute intervals, until it's all used up. Add more water to the pan whenever it dries up.

5. When the ham reaches an internal temperature of 160 degrees on a meat thermometer, remove ham and allow to rest for 15 minutes before carving.

SERVES ABOUT 24 IN A BUFFET WITH OTHER MAIN DISHES.

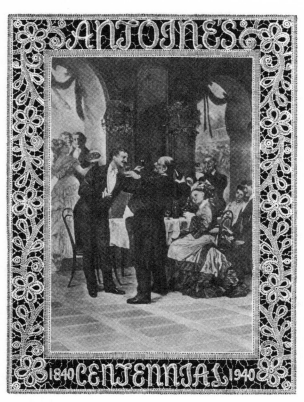

Antoine's menu from 1975. It's all in French, with 238 dishes listed. The cover was created for the centennial in 1940 and is still in use.

CHAPTER ELEVEN

Appetites Return

THE MENU IN THE MESS

The first morning I awakened again in my home, I walked around my few inexpensive rural acres to survey the damage. All the trees looked bare, even though early October in New Orleans doesn't qualify as fall. The lawn was high with weeds, but so much debris from the surrounding woods had blown over it that picking up the sticks alone would take days. I counted twenty-eight trees down, of which one had grazed the side of my house (doing only insignificant damage).

Mainly what I did while walking around was to try to mentally prepare for what I had planned that afternoon. I would go into town and try to get my head around that much worse situation. New Orleans was now wide open, although many parts of it were under curfew and even larger areas still had no power.

My neighbor Lee warned me about something I wouldn't have expected: terrific traffic snarls on the North Shore. So many people had moved over there—particularly from wiped-out St. Bernard Parish—that it now took an hour to make a trip that used to take ten minutes. The influx of St. Bernardians was so great that the large Catholic high school in Chalmette (the major town in the parish) had to relocate its campus fifty miles away, to the other side of the lake. That's where most of its students now lived.

Traffic was indeed heavy all the way across the Lake Pontchartrain Causeway, twenty-four miles spanning open water. It was the only major lake crossing in which Katrina had not opened gaps. The cars were also snarled pretty badly through Metairie, but when I took the fork in the I-10 into Orleans Parish, I suddenly found four open lanes. It was like six o'clock in the morning on Christmas—nobody coming, nobody going. I slowed down. There, on railings and light poles and everything else sticking up, were the soon-to-be-familiar horizontal lines showing how high the flood had gone. The expressway had been under several feet of water.

I exited at the Superdome. My one-room office of the past fifteen years was in a converted warehouse across the street from the stadium. Because thousands of desperate people crammed into it to escape the flood, the Superdome was on television a lot after the hurricane. I knew from that coverage that it had been surrounded by water at least waist-high. The flood in my office reached four and a half feet. The building had already been gutted. My stuff was gone—it had all dissolved into a heap of unsalvageable debris. All my past publications, photographs, and radio tapes—thirty years' worth—were gone forever. For a moment, I had that free feeling again. I wouldn't have to drag all that stuff around with me for the rest of my life. Then I had another thought: If this is my greatest material loss from the storm (and it was), then by the standards of my fellow citizens, I was lucky indeed. My luck had to be shared somehow.

I drove around town gingerly (you had to, because nails, glass shards, and other forms of debris were scattered widely on every street) for a couple of hours. Although I had already had a good idea of the extent of the damage, seeing it up close was a mind-bender. The abandoned cars alone did that job. It was necessary to have my mind bent, though, to relate to the people I would encounter who had put up with all this when conditions were much worse.

I met many such people in the following weeks. They were close and not-so-close friends, people I worked with, and relatives. And no small number of the strangers who come to know a person who works in the media. They all felt we had enough in common for them to just walk up and start talking (not that I ever minded that).

The moods ranged from optimism to depression. But they all had in common a fatalism I'd never encountered before in so many people at the same time. We were all coming to grips with the idea that the dreams and goals we had before the hurricane were now irrelevant. Before we could even start thinking about the future, we had to recover from this forced retreat into the past. That was such an overwhelming challenge that you couldn't even think about it in one piece; you could only take on a little part of it, and try to ignore the rest.

I ran into Mayor C. Ray Nagin at the radio station a couple of weeks after I came back to town. I asked him, "So, how's it going?" He looked into the corner of the ceiling, gave a helpless-looking smile, and said, "One day at a time!" While I was hoping for something more dynamic and imaginative from New Orleans's chief executive, I have to admit he was right in step with how all of his constituents felt.

The day of my first look at post-Katrina New Orleans headed toward a dusk that pulled a very dark night behind it. I turned toward home. When I passed in front of Andrea's, I thought I'd better check in. I was hungry, come to think of it. Chef Andrea—who worked in hotels for decades before he started his own place, and so was accustomed to the idea of remaining open all the time—had been open since mid-September. We exchanged the Katrina hug in a dining room whose carpets were gone, revealing a concrete floor. Unfinished wallboard was nailed to wall studs you could still see here and there. Nevertheless, Chef Andrea had a full house of customers. And that was only because it was early. By the time I left, people were stacked up in the bar, waiting for tables.

Chef Andrea opened a bottle of Cesari Amarone for us to share and launched into his tale of woe. His house got it as bad as the restaurant had. The same foot of water. He was up in arms, as many Metairie people were, about the way the parish abandoned the critical pumping stations during the storm. I told him he was lucky the water stood for only a day or two here, unlike the four or five (or six or seven) feet that sat stagnant for three weeks in Orleans Parish.

His most pitiable moaning, however, concerned his employees. He didn't have nearly enough of them to serve the number of diners who wanted to dine in his restaurant. The staff that day was an assortment of old pros and not-so-old, not-so-pros from other restaurants. No uniforms. The maître d' wore denim overalls and a hunting shirt. A couple of chefs from other restaurants wore the white jackets of their home kitchens.

"My pastry chef of almost twenty years left me," said Chef Andrea. "He told me he could make a lot more money working in construction." I would hear that story about many other former restaurant employees in the months to follow.

The menu was limited that night. I had veal Romano—like Wiener schnitzel, but with a red sauce. A bowl of turtle soup. It was good enough, but not up to Andrea's typical standards. I expected that, but I worried about it. Our city's usual level of culinary excellence certainly would be compromised for some time. Would some jerk food critic from somewhere else swoop in too soon and say New Orleans wasn't what it used to be?

I hung around Andrea's for a few hours. Many people invited me to join them at their tables; many Katrina hugs were exchanged, even with numerous people I'd never met in my life. Two themes emerged from the stories these people told. At most tables of two or more couples, one had lost their house in Lakeview or Mid-City or Gentill, and was staying in the damaged but livable Metairie home of the other. The other leitmotif was that all of these people were laughing, telling stories, toasting one another, and otherwise having what appeared to be a celebration. When I tuned in and listened to what they were saying, the real nature of their festivity came out. They were unloading stress. They were relieved to have returned to a beat-up lifestyle that was nevertheless recognizable and still in one piece, and they took as much of it as they could to convince themselves that the world had not ended.

Before the dinner rush, Chef Andrea and I planned an Eat Club dinner for the following week. What better way to demonstrate that the New Orleans food scene was alive and well than to resume Eat Club evenings? Even without the benefit of the radio show to promote the dinner (I got the word out through the Web site), we sold it out, to about forty diners, in less than a week. We had five courses in a room with unpainted wallboard, no carpets, and stackable chairs. The menu:

    Antipasto Misto
    Shrimp Caprese
    Fresh Pasta Marinara, Alfredo, and Pesto
    Red Snapper Basilico
    Tiramisu

All the fish was fresh and local, which seemed like a miracle at the time. Even as we told one another our Katrina stories—some of which were heart-stopping—not a long face was to be seen. The price for attending this dinner was whatever people wanted to pay, with any excess over what Chef Andrea charged going to a fund for displaced restaurant workers. More money went to the charity than to the restaurant. The food was terrific, and the loving mood was overwhelming.

Then came the e-mail from the concerned strangers who wanted me to join them at Restaurant August. That dinner was, for me, the confirmation of an idea that took root in my mind from the moment I arrived back in town: Not only would the culinary imperative of New Orleanians survive Katrina, but it would be one of the strongest forces pulling the city back together again.

I wrote the following words about this reassuring power. They were quoted in at least two other post-Katrina books I know of, so I may as well use them in my own:

> New Orleans's greatest asset is its uniqueness. We must maintain that at all costs. It is what makes people love our town . . . and, often, know more about the city than the locals do. These people will not break faith with us.
>
> We have a few things to do.
>
> 1. We must believe in a bright future. We must maintain the image of the unique culinary culture of New Orleans, both here and elsewhere. Let the world know that we'll be back, and that they'll have something they've never tasted in their lives waiting for them.
>
> 2. We must organize and plan. The restaurants and diners of our city need to communicate, create a plan for a big renaissance, and come back with the biggest culinary special event in the history of our country.
>
> Say it, and it becomes true. I say the serious eaters of the world cannot live without New Orleans food. And that when we give it to them again, it will be the best we've ever cooked.

Some of my readers replied to that and other hopeful pieces of mine with a much less sanguine outlook. How could I blame them? There was surely loads of evidence that rebuilding would be the battle of our lives.

THE FESTIVALS

For a lot of returned New Orleanians, a vital sign of the city's recovery from the hurricane was the resumption of its food-filled festivals.

Hardly a weekend goes by without a festival celebrating some element of local culture. There's always much food to be had. Not just hot dogs and popcorn, but the full menu of local eating, often cooked by restaurant chefs. Many of the festivals celebrate food per se. These include (to name but a few) the Gumbo Festival (several of those, actually), Crawfish Festival, Andouille Festival, Greek Festival, Oyster Festival, Jambalaya Festival, Crab Festival, and the unlikely but long-running Shrimp and Petroleum Festival.

Thousands of people show up for each of these, with eating as their primary goal. And these are the smaller ones. The big festivals go on for weeks and shut down parts of the city.

Here's a list of the festivals, with an emphasis on the ones with the best food.

January 6, the Epiphany, or **King's Day** is the official start of the Carnival season. It lasts through Mardi Gras (the day before Ash Wednesday), with the pitch of celebration rising as it goes.

Mardi Gras is the definitive New Orleans festival. It runs at full tilt for at least the two weeks before Ash Wednesday. Mardi Gras parades fill the streets not only in the city itself but throughout the suburbs and even into some exurban towns. Mardi Gras is not famous for its food, but it does have a distinctive local icon: the king cake, a circular, sweet yeast bread decorated in Mardi Gras colors of purple, green, and gold.

New Orleanians get tired of Lent quickly. **St. Joseph's Day, March 19** and the week around it, bring parades and the unique St. Joseph's altars. Those are set up in homes and restaurants, and seem to be constructed entirely of food.

Next, in the second weekend of April, comes the **French Quarter Festival**, with food and music scattered throughout the namesake historic district. The organization that puts this on also does the Satchmo Festival, a smaller but growing weekend August event that has more emphasis on music than food. The same organization offers the Reveillon (more on that later) in December. The schedules for all are at fqfi.com.

The last weekend in April and the first one in May bring the **New Orleans Jazz and Heritage Festival**, which is now almost as big as Mardi Gras. Although music is the centerpiece, the food is every bit as great a draw.

The week before Memorial Day is the **New Orleans Wine and Food Experience**, the most sophisticated food festival of all. Its tastings of chef-prepared dishes and hundreds of wines have grown so large that only the Superdome is big enough to hold it anymore.

That weekend is shared with the **Greek Festival**, which is extraordinary. Although New Orleans has never had many Greek restaurants, the Greek Orthodox community (the oldest in America) is large and enthusiastic. It seems that every Greek in town comes to this, and the food is marvelous, especially the pastries and the whole roasted lamb. Specialty food festivals continue through June, and start trailing off as the heat rises.

The year ends with the month-long **Reveillon**, in which some 40 restaurants offer holiday-themed dinners at attractive prices. This is the revival of a 200-year-old Creole holiday tradition. For many locals, it wouldn't be Christmas without attending one or more Reveillon dinners. I have the menus posted with my recommendations at http://www.nomenu.com/christmas.

King's Day	January 6
Mardi Gras	The day before Ash Wednesday
St. Joseph's Day	March 19
French Quarter Festival	Second week in April
New Orleans Jazz and Heritage Festival	Last weekend in April and first weekend in May
New Orleans Wine and Food Experience	The week before Memorial Day
Greek Festival	Memorial Day weekend
Reveillon	The month of December

Few places caught more of the brunt of the storm than Plaquemines Parish. That's just south of New Orleans, on the narrow neck of land that hugs the Mississippi River in its final miles before it reaches the Gulf of Mexico. In early November, two and a half months after the hurricane, the Louisiana Seafood Marketing Board organized an industry and media excursion to Empire, the center of the parish's vast oyster-producing area. Empire was also the first place Hurricane Katrina landed in Louisiana.

Representatives of commercial fishing interests—the oyster guys, the shrimpers, the seafood dealers—related their plight as the bus made its way down. The boats, the docks, the processing plants, the icehouses, and every other part of their livelihoods were either severely damaged or gone completely.

The citrus stands, which that time of year would usually be filled with Plaquemines oranges and satsumas, were all closed. But the orange groves themselves looked okay. Just a few trees down, lots of oranges on the ground. The houses and other structures didn't look especially worse than what I'd seen elsewhere around town.

But just a minute or two past this scene, we reached a police checkpoint. Identification as a resident was required for anyone to go any farther, and even then you had to be out of the area by dark. We would soon see why. Our police escort led us to the old highway that runs next to the river levee and into a town called Diamond.

The destruction in Diamond was an order of magnitude—perhaps two—worse than anything I'd seen so far. Nearly every house was off its foundation, placed at strange angles to the road. A large oyster truck was hanging from a tree, a few feet off the ground. Everything was wrecked beyond any dream of repair. And it went on like that for miles.

"That was Ground Zero," one of the fishermen said. "When you get to Empire, you'll see Ground Sub-zero." This was no exaggeration. In Empire, boats were on top of houses. Houses on top of trees. Quite a few houses were half a block away and across the street from their addresses. And those were the ones that were still in one piece. Many houses were now just boards scattered all over the place.

The most bizarre spectacle of all involved the fishing boats. They were strewn all over dry land. The ones still in the water were in insane tangles with one another. Two gigantic "pogy boats"—vessels that scoop up menhaden, the fish used for cat food—had been carried by the storm surge halfway up a high-rise overpass. They were now parked there, seeming to ask, "So what in the hell are you going to do about *this*?" Strangely, what most of us did was laugh. It was like a scene out of a movie with very heavy special effects.

My friend Harlon Pearce was along for this tour of Empire. He's in the seafood wholesale business and he lost a million dollars' worth of fish when the power went off during the storm at the cold storage warehouse. "I'd tell you what it was like to clean that up, but really, the quarter million pounds of chicken in there was even worse."

I did my best to compute all this on the trip back to Metairie. There, the group lunched at the Acme Oyster House. We started with, of all things, raw oysters on the half shell. The Seafood Marketing Board guys got up and explained that, despite what we'd just seen, there was plenty of Louisiana seafood out there. And that it was not only without taint (all the authorities vouched for that), but of unusually excellent quality. Shrimp and crabmeat especially. The oysters were certainly fine.

This was a pleasant surprise, two months after hearing predictions that it would be years before we'd eat Louisiana oysters again. In fact, I had had my first oysters a couple of weeks earlier, when Dickie Brennan and I had hesitated for a moment before devouring the first oysters to arrive at his Bourbon House since the storm.

RELUCTANT RETURNEES

On my way home from the Empire expedition, I got a call from Mary Ann. She and Mary Leigh were on the fourth and final day of their long-delayed return home—about 200 miles away. They would stop at Leatha's, the barbecue joint they like in Hattiesburg.

This was good, I thought. I could get home, take a shower and a nap, and make something special—chocolate mousse, which they love—to greet my girls on their homecoming.

They were charmed by my mousse, the flowers, the clean house, and some other gifts. But the charm didn't overcome their discomfort in the environment formerly known as home. All those trees on the ground. And all those gaps and broken branches in the trees that had managed to remain upright. The ripped-up buildings. The dead power lines snaking across roads everywhere. They were talking about going back to Washington before the evening ended. They didn't—not right away.

Meanwhile, back in DC, my son Jude was thriving as a boarding student at Georgetown Prep. After the holidays, Mary Leigh resumed her freshman year at the Academy of the Sacred Heart, an excellent school she'd chosen herself two years earlier. But it wasn't the same for her. Part of the problem was having to pass through a large devastated area of the city to get to school every morning. How could she not compare that with the beautiful Stone Ridge Academy, the school that had taken her in following our evacuation to Washington? After a few months, although her grades stayed at their usual top level, she could no longer handle going to Sacred Heart. Or living in New Orleans. She and Mary Ann moved back to Washington. They rented an apartment, and Mary Leigh finished the school year at Stone Ridge—which not only welcomed her back but gave her and two other New Orleans girls an award for courage at the commencement. They remained in DC for most of the next school year.

I remained in New Orleans alone. What else could I do? I needed to get back to work. Mary Ann felt that I hadn't given the idea of living in DC permanently a chance. But, given the extreme specialization of what I do, I would never be able to earn the money in any other city that I did in New Orleans—at least not in the short term. And once it became clear to me not only that I could continue my career successfully in New Orleans, but that I was playing a role in the recovery, leaving town became anathema.

Many New Orleans families had to deal with this issue. Businesses and jobs were moving out of town, taking with them a lot of people who really didn't want to move. Many families were split, both physically and emotionally—sometimes permanently. As of this writing we seem to be doing OK. One day at a time, to quote the mayor.

BURGEONING

By the post-Katrina three-month mark, my New Orleans Restaurant Index had zoomed past 200, even with vast areas of the city still uninhabitable by either restaurants or their customers. Restaurants were opening right and left. The ones that had already opened were doing such overwhelming business that many others—including no small number of brand-new ones—were motivated to get into the act.

As I noted earlier, the first major restaurants that reopened were reluctant to serve gourmet dishes, offering home-style cooking instead. That didn't last long, not only because their customers wanted the chefs' real food, but also because plenty of home-style restaurants were already back open to serve that hunger. (We all wanted to eat our red beans, but not when we went to Restaurant August or Emeril's.) In fact, the small neighborhood cafés soon constituted a majority of the restaurants on the Index. The margin has continued to widen. There's never been a time when New Orleans had so many poor boy shops, blue-plate-special cafés, and other neighborhood eateries. Or so many ethnic restaurants, particularly in the Asian category.

I had a hard time persuading visiting journalists of that statistic, however. Their first question always seemed to be, "So, the famous restaurants in the French Quarter are coming back, but it's a real shame about all the mom-and-pop places washed away by Katrina, isn't it?" When I told them that the situation was, in fact, the other way around—that the French Quarter places, facing years of much-reduced tourism, were in far greater peril—they hardly knew what to say next. Some of them repeated the question, trying to get me to agree with their a priori conclusion that the little restaurants surely were doomed. I pointed them to my Index, which included names, addresses, and phone numbers for all the restaurants, in case they wanted to check out my assertion that the corner cafés were thriving.

The most inspiring example of that comeback was what happened in the large Vietnamese community in New Orleans East. The storm surge didn't need a levee break to do its damage there. It rolled right over the levees and pushed ten or more feet of water across the entire area. What's more, that part of town was much closer to the eye of the storm and its maximum winds. It was a wipeout.

NEW ORLEANS RESTAURANT CENSUS AFTER KATRINA

Here are some notable numbers from The New Orleans Menu Restaurant Index, published since shortly after the hurricane. Excluded from all counts are fast-food, delivery-only, take-out-only, and institutional spots, and anywhere else food is not cooked on-site. It does include local sandwich shops and other neighborhood cafés.

Restaurants open in the New Orleans metropolitan area, August 26, 2005 (the day before the Katrina evacuation began): 809

Restaurants open August 30, 2005: 0.

Restaurants open January 1, 2006: 401.

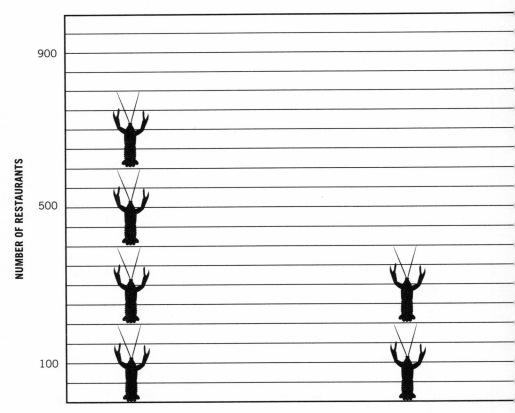

NUMBER OF RESTAURANTS

900

500

100

First ten major restaurants to reopen after Hurricane Katrina, in alphabetical order. (The actual opening dates are hard to figure, since many restaurants began cooking rudimentary meals well before opening for regular service.) All these were open by the first week of October 2005.

Andrea's
Bacco
Cuvée
Dakota
Drago's
Le Parvenu
Red Fish Grill
Restaurant August
Rib Room
Zea

Restaurants open a year after the hurricane: 680.

Date on which as many restaurants were open as before the hurricane: April 16, 2007.

Restaurants open three years after the hurricane: 955.

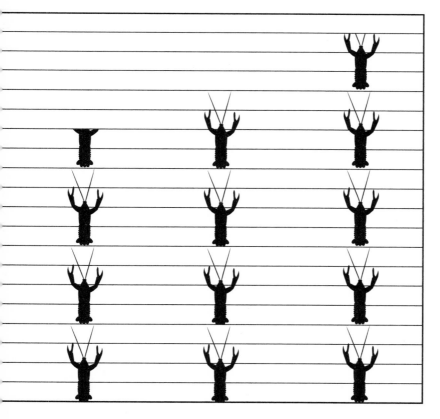

Fans of the neighborhood's cuisine were most upset about Dong Phuong, a restaurant beloved not only for its big menu of Viet dishes, but also for baking wonderful French bread for its poor boy–like banh mi sandwiches. We thought it was surely the end for that and the other restaurants out there in the East. Then, less than two months after the storm, we saw the first of the Vietnamese restaurants in the area reopen. That was soon followed by other businesses and the return of most of the residents. They just dug in and fixed things, not bothering to wait around for insurance settlements and government assistance. It wasn't what it had been—a burgeoning community of people farming, fishing, and selling the unique products of their culinary culture—but it was back in business.

The New Orleans dining puzzle had a lot of missing pieces, all right. But diversity, and even diversity of diversity, was not one of them. If you looked even a little, by the end of that awful year 2005 you could find any kind of restaurant that had been there before the storm.

BREATHING THE AIR

The week of the Marys' temporary return brought another resumption of life as I had known it. WWL Radio asked me to return to the air that weekend. The logistics, by necessity, were rather peculiar. The owners of our badly damaged building next to the Superdome wouldn't allow us back in. For many weeks, we shared the facilities and personnel of our most strident competitors, in the studios of their affiliates in Baton Rouge. This meant a ninety-minute commute each way to do the radio show. But I was relieved, and eager to do it.

The host who preceded me said, "Is this your first show back? Wow. Get ready. You're not going to believe what you're going to hear. These people are out of their minds with rage."

"I'm not going to get into any of that stuff," I said. "I'm going to do a food show, just like always."

"You won't get away with it," he said. "They want to cut heads off, and you can't stop them. Even the sports guys are talking about FEMA and the Corps of Engineers and all that."

I opened the mike and explained my intentions. I gave the latest number of restaurants open, named the ones that had recently returned, and asked about any eateries the listeners may have visited. And, I wanted to know, if you're back home but your kitchen is a mess, what are you cooking, and how? If you have a wine collection, how did it fare? And other stuff like that.

The first caller was convincing. "*Thank God* we can stop talking about levee breaks and insurance problems!" he said. "We're sick of hearing about that twenty-four hours a day! I'm so happy to hear your voice! Now—when is Commander's Palace going to reopen?" Here was someone who agreed that food could heal us.

Everyone else who called during the next four hours felt the same way, save for one caller who tried to sneak in with a flood-insurance complaint. For the next month, I did shows of between four and six hours every Friday, Saturday, and Sunday. I received no more hurricane-distress calls. Even more reassuring, nobody called to demand that this frivolous gourmet stuff be taken off the air while so many people were still suffering. It was great to learn that even stressed New Orleanians could still compartmentalize. Either that, or they knew that without our cooking, music, and the rest of our local culture, we were of little value to anyone.

By December 2005, the radio station was back in New Orleans, and I was back on the air every day on WSMB. The management liked having at least a little optimism on WWL, whose other shows remained full of desperation and anger. They kept me on the air there on Saturdays. Three years later, I'm still doing that extra show on the big-gun station.

Working in our old studios was disturbing. We were the only occupants in the formerly full twenty-six-story building. The building was missing about half of its windows and no longer had regular janitorial service. Trash and leaves blew around in the lobby. Sometimes the power or the water went out. It was like a scene from an Armageddon movie, with a few survivors huddled in an abandoned skyscraper. We didn't move to new quarters until more than a year has passed, and I was the last host to move to the new digs. That was my version of moving out of a FEMA trailer and back into a real house.

Whole Flounder Stuffed with Crabmeat

Bruning's opened at West End Park in 1859 and remained popular and excellent, run by the same family, until it and everything else at West End was destroyed by Hurricane Katrina. Bruning's great specialty was stuffed whole flounder. The restaurant may be gone (although maybe not forever), but the dish lives on. Use the biggest flounder you can find. (Fishermen refer to those as "doormats.") I use claw crabmeat for the stuffing, because it has a more pronounced taste.

Stuffing
½ stick butter
¼ cup flour
3 green onions, chopped
3 cups shrimp stock
1 Tbs. Worcestershire sauce
1 lb. claw crabmeat (or crawfish, in season)
¼ tsp. salt
Pinch cayenne
Flounder
4 large whole flounder
1 Tbs. salt-free Creole seasoning
1 tsp. salt
1 cup flour
2 eggs
1 cup milk
½ cup clarified butter
1 lemon, sliced
Fresh parsley, chopped

Preheat overn to 400 degrees.

1. Make the stuffing first. Melt the butter, and stir in the flour to make a blond roux. Stir in the green onions, and cook until limp. Whisk in the shrimp stock and Worcestershire, and bring to a boil, then add the crabmeat, salt, and cayenne. Gently toss the crabmeat in the sauce to avoid breaking the lumps.

2. Wash the flounder and pat dry. Mix the Creole seasoning and salt into the flour, and coat the outside of the flounder with it. Mix the eggs and milk together in a wide bowl, and pass the fish through it, then dredge in the seasoned flour again.

3. Heat the clarified butter in a skillet and sauté the fish, one at a time, about four minutes on each side, turning once. Remove and keep warm.

4. Cut a slit from head to tail across the top of each flounder. Divide stuffing among the fish, spooning inside it the slit and piling it on top. Place the flounder on an ungreased baking pan, and put into the preheated oven for six minutes.

5. Place the flounder on hot plates. Garnish with lemon slices and fresh chopped parsley.

SERVES FOUR TO EIGHT.

The New Orleans Underground Gourmet

Where to find great meals in New Orleans for less than $3.75 and as little as 50c.

BY RICHARD H. COLLIN

The first edition of Richard Collin's restaurant guide, which inspired me to explore the restaurant scene and write about it.

CHAPTER TWELVE

Back to Abnormal

The Spirited People

New Orleans couldn't wait for 2005 to end. But the disastrous year would not say die. Tropical storms kept forming in the Atlantic and Gulf right past the end of the hurricane season and beyond. Although they all bypassed New Orleans in the end, with the city's defenses at their weakest, they freaked us out. On New Year's Eve, for God's sake, the region saw the first named Atlantic tropical storm in history cross over into a brand-new year: Tropical Storm Zeta (they'd run out of names a few storms ago, and were now using Greek letters). It was the most active season on record by far, leaving quite a few records broken.

So everybody in New Orleans was still on edge at year's end. But the tension took two very different forms. Some of us felt we were in hell, and were looking for an escape from it. But just as many thought we were . . . well, not in heaven, but at least back to a familiar place on earth. And, all in all, it was a good place.

There were thousands of people whose homes had been destroyed, whose insurance companies were refusing to pay up, whose jobs were gone, whose schools would never reopen, who were unable to return home, or who lost family or friends. And there were thousands of reasons to be livid with anger after Hurricane Katrina. The institutions that make a community function had failed wholesale. How could they be trusted in the future?

Many books (both fiction and nonfiction), articles, television shows, and movies have been written about the total breakdown of nearly everything right after the storm, and about the permanent harm that came to hundreds of thousands of people. The worst-hit victims got most of the attention in these investigations, as well they should have. But many of the people who suffered major losses were eager to put all that behind them, work as hard as they had to in order to repair their homes and businesses, and in the end return to their highly unpromising city.

You couldn't call these people cheerful, but they were optimistic. They were accepting of the challenge before them, but not fatalistic. Dissatisfied, but not furious. Although New Orleans was depicted by the media as a city of desperate people, many of these optimistic citizens were possessed with a desire to resume the New Orleans life as they'd known it. And when they set out to let the good times roll again, they found the same encouraging phenomenon that I did: plenty of others who felt the same way. And when all those people got together, the delicious times commenced with enthusiasm. It was something to live for.

Most of these optimistic spirits had disasters to deal with. Don and Andrea Smith, a couple with whom we became friends when our sons attended Jesuit High School, are one example. The Smiths lived in Lakeview. They were well along in renovating their house when the levee broke and sent a river nine feet deep of brown, oily water through their house. For two years, the Smiths had to live in Baton Rouge while trying to do something about that mess. They ultimately gave up and sold the old house. But they built a new one—in Lakeview, yet. In the meantime, they were always ready to have dinner with me in the months that my family was absent. They came to many Eat Club dinners. They clearly relished the good times they arranged for themselves.

People like the Smiths told their stories of Katrina-engendered woe. But they shrugged their shoulders instead of cursing their fate. Most of them even laughed about it, as they ate and drank more or less as they had before, in grand restaurants and neighborhood joints.

Yes, the people who lost all their resources had an appalling story to tell and needed the support of the rest of us. But if the rest of us hadn't come back to administer CPR to the collective New Orleans lifestyle, how could the city ever have returned to consciousness? What would New Orleans be without food? Music? Fun? Why would tourists and conventioneers—the customers of the city's largest industry—come to town if there were nothing delicious to draw them? Even though some of the tour companies made a good business out of tours through the devastated areas, pity is not an emotion many people travel in order to experience.

The spirited people of New Orleans inspired the restaurateurs to come back, and vice-versa. The way Orleanians poured into the reopened restaurants encouraged those that hadn't opened yet to get a move on. The early comers made a lot of money. It could also be said that if the restaurants hadn't come back so quickly, a lot of people who returned to town wouldn't have; that certainly would have made a difference to me.

I don't think we'll ever again experience a time like fall 2005, when almost everything was a wreck. It was like the Summer of Love; everyone you ran into embraced you. Even people who didn't particularly like each other forgave everything and exchanged the Katrina hug. I certainly had my share of such experiences. The fomenter of a Web message board largely dedicated to attacking me wrote to say that she wanted to apologize; I wrote back to accept and apologize for whatever it was I had said or done to set her off. The enmity ended there, permanently. Most people I knew told of similar reconciliations.

You had to be in New Orleans at that time to know how deep this euphoria ran, and the degree to which it cleansed our spirits. People who weren't here—or who were obsessed with exploring every bit of the hell that lay around them—find the post-Katrina spirit hard to understand or even believe. A fool's paradise. My assertion that good cooking was fixing a lot of things was derided by some as preposterous.

But it wasn't. It was real, and realistic. And very effective in its power to heal.

HIGHS AND LOWS

On the other hand, like all other good things, the joie de vivre could be overdone. Since many of us weren't working, we could go to lunch and not worry about having to get back. Wine and liquor distributors told me they had never seen a time when local people drank so much. In a city where it's been said that if you die of cirrhosis of the liver it's considered natural causes, that's saying something. It was like what happens to a lot of college freshmen when they're finally on their own for the first time.

I know it was happening to me. I remember in particular a lunch with a longtime friend in the public relations business and two of her friends, two months after the storm. It was in the Royal Orleans Hotel's Rib Room, which had just reopened to celebrate its forty-fifth anniversary. (The hotel, in the center of the French Quarter, was the headquarters of the New Orleans Police Department during the weeks after the storm and kept operations up—but not for the general public.)

At lunch, none of us had a foot even close to the brake pedal. The lunch rivaled in length and excess the ones I used to have with Dick Brennan; we stayed until dinner. So did most of the other people in the room. It's no surprise that there was a spike in incidences of alcoholism in Louisiana that year. It's a common phenomenon in the wake of major disasters.

Many other forces kept us sober, however. All you had to do was drive around. A banker I knew often took people on a tour of the devastation. At the end of it, he'd say, "We have driven forty-five miles. Not one of the houses we passed has people living in it." If you wanted to wallow, it was easy enough.

One night on my way home, I drove up Canal Street, the grand main boulevard of New Orleans. The floodwater had covered most of the street's length, from the edge of the French Quarter all the way out to the historic cemeteries at the end of the streetcar line. The streetcars themselves—brand-new replicas of our 1920s-vintage classics, put into service only two years earlier—had all succumbed to the flood.

Nor was anything else in working order as I drove through the darkness. A few lights, powered by generators or batteries, shone from houses in the darkness, but the neighboring homes were largely uninhabitable and vacant. No traffic lights or streetlights. The only illumination to speak of came from the headlights of the few other cars.

At the cemeteries, access to the I-10 was blocked that night. I knew an alternate route, through the Lakeview section. I wasn't far along when I found myself in an area where the darkness made Canal Street look like Mardi Gras by comparison; not a single light or sign of life was visible in any direction. Even though I was very familiar with the neighborhood, it was frightening. The weight of the deep water that had stood in Lakeview for so long actually buckled most of its streets into shallow roller coasters.

My headlights panned across gray houses with open doors. There was nothing worth protecting; everything inside was covered with mud, mold, or both. If thieves invaded and took something away, they'd be doing the owners a favor. The only other cars were the silt-covered vehicles lining the streets and parked in driveways, nevermore to move under their own power. It looked like a scene from an apocalyptic movie. Eerie. Depressing. Everything dead, dead, dead.

"THE NEIGHBORHOOD NEEDS ME"

In the months right after the hurricane, all the debris collected throughout the city was brought to the long park that bisects Lakeview. There it was piled higher than any other mound in the history of the city. It went on for about ten blocks. It was amazing to look at. Actually drew tourists.

On an afternoon a week or so after she returned to town, I collected my daughter from school. We wanted to have dinner, but we had time to kill first. She wanted to take a look at Debris Mountain to see how high it was now. Fifty or sixty feet, we estimated. After checking that out, we turned into the neighborhood so I could see how bad things were at Tony Angello's, one of the city's most popular Italian restaurants. It was just a few blocks from the levee break and had water so high that when the emergency personnel went through the neighborhood in their boats, they had to inscribe their orange X on Tony Angello's roof, rather than its walls.

When I got there, except for the many dead trees (saltwater does that), the restaurant looked superficially as it had before the storm. And there, standing in front, was Tony Angello himself. I parked and hailed him. We exchanged the Katrina hug.

"Tom, I'm glad you're all right," he said. "And I want to invite you inside for dinner. I want to—but I can't. Let me show you why." We went inside the formerly charming antique dining room, and he waved his arm across it. There was nothing there now but bare concrete floors and black studs.

Tony Angello was almost eighty at the time. Right after the storm, he was deeply depressed by what he saw. Like most people in Lakeview, he didn't have flood insurance. (The Feds said it was unnecessary, until after the flood.) At first, his thought was that this would be a logical time to hang it up. His mood went to the other side a few days later. "I have to open again, Tom," he told me. "My customers are begging me. The neighborhood needs me." This was no self-important boast. In the two years it took Mr. Tony to undo the effects of the deluge, few other restaurants engendered more on-air calls asking urgently about their future.

I heard the same words a few weeks later, at a conference held at Tulane University by the National Trust for Historic Preservation. The organization was concerned about the potentially enormous loss of historic buildings, sites, and institutions in New Orleans following the hurricane. The culinary culture was on their A-list. I moderated a panel of restaurateurs who reassured everyone that the food community was coming back very strong and that their customers were ecstatic to find it that way.

The most memorable presentation came from Leah Chase, known locally as the Queen of Creole Cooking, an encomium that's hard to deny. She started cooking in the 1940s, and her restaurant Dooky Chase is the Galatoire's of the New Orleans African-American community. After having written several definitive cookbooks on Creole-soul cooking and gaining much national recognition, when Leah Chase speaks on food she speaks for New Orleans.

Dooky Chase was deep in the flood zone and, like Tony Angello's and many others, was uninsured for floods. Miss Leah was well past eighty and had no resources with which to rebuild. But she's so well liked and respected that several organizations—most from out of town—came to her aid, allowing her to repair and reopen her restaurant.

That deal wasn't yet done when she gave her side of the story at Tulane. Thoughtful, knowledgeable, and articulate, Miss Leah explained why Creole cooking is essential to the life of New Orleans. She described her own hefty problems, and then spoke those words: "I have to reopen for the sake of my neighborhood. If I don't open, my neighborhood won't come back." Everybody nodded. Her neighborhood needed her.

Surely some must have thought this was a chicken-and-egg puzzle. Neighborhoods without people could surely not support restaurants, could they? Maybe not anywhere else, but in New Orleans, yes, they could. The panel members and locals in the audience had no trouble thinking of restaurants that were for months the only permanent signs of life in their neighborhoods. East New Orleans—in terms of square miles the largest area of total devastation, and predominantly black middle-class—had a barbecue joint, a seafood house, and a few poor boy shops before any significant number of people were back in their houses. All had lines of customers. These were not just hungry construction workers. No sooner had they opened than people were calling me on the air to say how good they were.

CRITICAL MASS

On December 29, the third-to-last day of that year of horrors, I was on my way back from yet another lunch with kindred spirits in the French Quarter when I noticed the delivery door at Antoine's was open. Why? I wondered. With all the damage it sustained from the storm, I knew the main building was in no shape to open soon; there was still some question as to whether it ever would.

I entered the long, narrow hallway, hoping someone at the other end would recognize me and know I wasn't a looter. I found a half dozen waiters in civilian attire and fifth-generation Antoine descendant Michael Guste. Katrina hugs were over now, so it was handshakes all around.

"What's happening?" I asked.

"We're opening tonight," Michael said.

I couldn't believe it. "Do you have a table for four available?"

"We already have 200 booked, and we don't want to stress the kitchen," he said, then laughed. "But I guess we can get you in."

He showed me around. The main dining room still looked precarious, its ceiling propped up by temporary supports. "We caught it just in time, before it all caved in," said Michael. Then we passed through the Annex, Antoine's largest and most popular dining room. It's in a different building and had no serious damage. We wound up in the wine cellar, one of the most striking visuals in any restaurant anywhere. It's a hall that extends seemingly to the horizon. Its racks were empty. "Everything in there was ruined by the heat after the storm." I'd heard that story before.

The scene when I returned for dinner at seven o'clock was reminiscent of those in the first restaurants that opened after the storm. The Katrina hug was back in circulation. Everybody was giddy to be dining at Antoine's under any circumstances—even with the limited menu, the absence of some old waiters, the soufflé potatoes being served on a tray instead of in a basket made of woven potatoes, and a bunch of other compromises that would have been intolerable pre-Katrina.

Rick Blount, another of Antoine's great-great-grandsons and the family member now in charge, introduced himself. He wore a sheepish smile. "You can't imagine what this has been like," he said. "We weren't sure we could start this machine back up again after it sat here four months with a gaping hole in its side. But so far only one thing has gone wrong. The very first cocktail order. A Champagne cocktail. The bartender reached up for a sugar cube, and it wasn't there. The one thing we forgot to order, that's the first thing somebody wanted."

Three days later, with a much more flamboyant alacrity, Galatoire's reopened. The restaurant had been in the throes of celebrating its one hundredth anniversary when Katrina hit, and both the restaurant and its regular customers were primed to resume it. Galatoire's sustained no physical damage of note from the storm, but having the power out for three weeks created evil new life forms inside its refrigerators. It was so bad that they decided to rip them all out and rebuild them from scratch—not easy, since everything in a building that old is a custom job.

Antoine's and Galatoire's are two of the four restaurants

considered the eternal verities of the French Quarter dining scene. The other two had equally good news to tell. Arnaud's was actually the first of them to reopen, early in December 2005, three months after Katrina. That made it the only one of the grande dames to be present through that holiday season—a time when New Orleanians traditionally flock to such old-style restaurants. Broussard's, the last of the four to open, just missed a 2005 return but was open two weeks into January 2006.

Important reopenings like those brought 2005 to a promising close. The restaurant count was up to 400—about half of the number open before the storm. The return of the New Orleans culinary world as a whole was no longer in doubt—in general.

In particular, though, things were often less promising. Commander's Palace had served people grandly since 1880, but it had to stop doing so for more than a year. "It's Pandora's box!" Lally Brennan told me. "Every time we fix one thing, six new things we didn't know about turn up!" Lally and her cousin Ti Martin had taken the reins of the Brennan family's flagship a couple of years before, allowing Ella and Dick Brennan to retire.

At first, they thought the hurricane damage to the old mansion that is Commander's was slight. But when they opened up a wall, they found not just mold but full-fledged, structure-compromising rot. The deeper they went, the worse it looked. The restoration cost many millions of dollars and wasn't finished until October 2006. The delay was so extreme and unexpected that a rumor spread that the Brennans were in trouble. They weren't, but a lot of people were ready to believe the worst in those days.

The frustrating year of reconstruction at Commander's did, however, have one positive effect. It exorcized a demon. In 2001, a horrible, fast-moving cancer killed Jamie Shannon, one of the most likable chefs in the history of New Orleans cooking. He was Emeril's successor at Commander's Palace and one of the authors of the First Tuesday dinners Marcelle Bienvenu and I had with Dick Brennan for ten years. Jamie was only forty when he died. He had little kids. His demise upset the Commander's team so much that they couldn't seem to regain their momentum. But when they finally got back to work after the storm, the karma was clearly back in balance. Jamie's successor, Tory McPhail, came on with strong, innovative menus and five-star haute Creole cooking again. Commander's has resumed its place as the standard-bearer for the city's gourmet restaurants.

At the end of 2006, 724 real restaurants were back open in New Orleans. That was just 85 shy of the number of restaurants before the hurricane. It was a long way to come in sixteen months after the kind of hit the city had suffered.

But it was a strain. The exile or permanent departure of all those people who had lived in all those uninhabitable houses (more than 250,000 people, more than 100,000 houses) left the New Orleans workforce critically weakened. The thousands of trailers that came to town after the storm helped, but only a little. Only people who had no other options lived in the trailers, which were small, bunched together in parks, and clearly only a stopgap measure.

Adding to the problem, a significant number of people who were in town were there strictly on what employers called "FEMAcation" or "hurrication." Only when the federal emergency money and free rent ran out did some people return to work. I wouldn't have believed this had not so many restaurateurs and other business owners told me the same story.

So the restaurants made do with far less staff than they had before. Some resorted to importing people from far away. Hispanic cooks—common in kitchens across America, but historically rare in New Orleans—were now on the lines in many restaurants. The Brennans brought in dozens of servers from Russia, of all places. They spoke English perfectly and were well versed in the art of dining room service. But their personalities were a lot different from the Cajun waiters. (Some of the Russian waiters were easier to understand than the Cajuns, though.)

Even the most forgiving diners noticed that service was not what it had been. There simply weren't enough experienced waiters in town. The restaurants jacked up pay scales to unheard-of heights to attract new people. But a new waiter or cook doesn't do the same job that an experienced one does. And the restaurants were so understaffed that the managers rarely had time to put the new people through a thorough training program.

Sommeliers had the similar problems with their wine cellars. You could buy 2003 Bordeaux to replace the 1983s whose corks popped in the post-Katrina heat wave—as hundreds of corks did. But it wasn't nearly as fine a wine. And there was absolutely nothing that could be done about that.

RESURRECTION FROM THE DEAD

In addition to the many reopenings, more brand-new restaurants opened in 2006 than in any year in recent memory. These generally weren't large, expensive projects, but quite a few were solidly in the gourmet category. Meanwhile, almost none of the reopened restaurants closed again. New Orleans, with all its problems, continued to enjoy a much lower rate of restaurant failures than any other major American city. (This remained true in the recession that began in 2008.)

Mr. B's Bistro reopened on May 16, 2007. By happy coincidence, that brought the population of open eateries up to 809—the exact number of restaurants open right before the storm. Mr. B's took so long to reopen because it had the bad luck to have a basement—one of the very few in New Orleans. The basement filled with water and caused all kinds of trouble. The parking garage overhead sprung a leak during the hurricane and created a Niagara into the middle of the kitchen. The wood floor buckled, requiring that the whole place be rebuilt from top to bottom.

Mr. B's was closed too long not to have lost its momentum. Although it brought back its chef, manager, and other key personnel, much of its staff had scattered. It had a tougher time than expected returning to its former excellence and popularity. A lot of its regular customers were out of the Mr. B's habit. Things did finally return to normal—the place is too good to ignore. But it was a close call.

Mr. B's was the last major restaurant to reopen—among those we were sure were coming back, anyway. On the other hand, some noteworthy establishments were gone for good. Their owners were getting on in years, or their buildings had been too badly damaged to rebuild, or they had intractable insurance problems. It's hard to fault them for this, particularly in the case of the older restaurateurs.

Without question the most heartbreaking quietus landed on

West End Park. West End began as a resort on the lake in the flush pre–Civil War years of New Orleans. The oldest restaurant there—Bruning's—had been in continuous operation since 1859. The unique selling proposition of the West End eateries was that they were built on stilts over the water, affording views of the lake. Eating seafood in a place like that was one of the most cherished of New Orleans dining traditions. It came to a full stop on August 29, though. Hurricane Katrina left absolutely nothing standing at West End. Boats from the nearby marina were scattered about like so much litter after a Mardi Gras parade. Because West End is outside the levee system, it's unlikely that the dozen or so restaurants that once stood there will ever be replaced.

The best restaurant in New Orleans to expire as a result of Katrina was Christian's. It was opened in 1972 by Henry Bergeron and Chris Ansel. (A member of the Galatoire family, Ansel worked for years at Galatoire's.) Christian's had terrific, original food (it invented the cold-smoked soft-shell crab, for example). But its premises were even more memorable: It was in a small, old church with a tall steeple. During the storm, Christian's was smack-dab in the middle of Mid-City's deep, long flood. Bergeron—who a few years earlier had bought out Ansel—was so upset by the damage that he couldn't bring himself to reopen. In 2008, he sold the restaurant. It was magnificent irony that the buyer was a church community.

Four blocks away from Christian's was Manuel's Hot Tamales. A relic of the 1940s, Manuel's was a shabby old storefront where peppery, alarmingly greasy little tamales were made and sold until the wee hours of the morning. The woman who ran it was up in years, and the flood filled the old stand to the ceiling and beyond, then sat there. As of this writing, Manuel's has not returned, and I doubt it will. But with each passing day the memory of those hot tamales becomes more delicious to many Orleanians—even those who hadn't been there for many years before the storm.

Locals also pine for Restaurant Mandich, a fine old neighborhood café with terrific food. Mandich had minimal flood damage, but it was on the road to the Ninth Ward and St. Bernard Parish, where most of its customers lived. All those people lost their homes, and then they were gone. Owner Lloyd English, his wife, and chef

Joel had run the place hands-on for decades. They were plenty old enough to retire, so they did. Still, not a week goes by that someone doesn't call or e-mail wishing Mandich would come back.

Then there were the Croziers. Gerard and Eveline Crozier had already retired once before, after operating the best French bistro in the annals of New Orleans dining for twenty-seven years. After a couple of years off, they came back with an excellent French-accented steakhouse, which had the bad luck to open right before 9/11. As soon as that blew over, construction on a new streetcar line cut off access to the restaurant for two years. When that was finished, mad cow disease broke out in Canada, doubling the price of beef. Finally, when Katrina left four feet of water in their dining room for three weeks, the Croziers surrendered and left town for Knoxville.

Really, though, it was surprising how few such stories there were. Even with the very soft tourism that New Orleans expected for the years after Katrina, business prospects for restaurants were good enough that few storm-forced closings were permanent. Even now, restaurants that once seemed irretrievably extinct continue to reopen under new owners, who see opportunities in the famous old names.

The most flagrant example of this is Charlie's Steak House. Founded in 1932 and renovated only once (after a 1967 fire forced the issue), the joint's only competition for sleaziest good restaurant in New Orleans was Uglesich's. Everything was insanely worn out. The walls and floors were covered with grease from the pools of sizzling steak butter that topped warped aluminum plates. Charlie's was a dump to end all arguments.

Two feet of Katrina floodwater found its way into and around Charlie's. The family that owned it had dwindled to two octogenarians. Charlie's just sat there dissolving in mildew for three years. Unlike most storm-damaged buildings, though, it didn't look particularly worse after the storm than before. How could it?

During those three years, more radio listeners and e-mail correspondents asked me about the fate of Charlie's than about any other restaurant. I heard the question at least once a day. It was an amazing phenomenon, considering that Charlie's was really a minor player on the dining scene. If all the people who asked me about

Charlie's had actually eaten there with frequency, you would never have been able to get into the place. But it hadn't been all that busy. This was just sleazy chic again, and the longer the old joint remained closed, the more alluring it became.

The savior of Charlie's was a neighbor who grew up eating there and wanted it back. His renovation, completed in 2008, kept many suggestions (but few realities) of the old sleaziness. Today, the warped plates are still sizzling with their monster steaks, but the place looks better than anyone can remember. When Charlie's was mobbed from day one, I knew what would happen next, and I was right. People called to tell me Charlie's wasn't like they remembered it. How could it be? Three years of experiencing Charlie's only through reminiscence could not be equaled by mere reality.

The story of Willie Mae's Scotch House was the mirror image of the Charlie's story. A block away from Dooky Chase, Willie Mae's was operated for forty years by Willie Mae Seaton, who at the time of Katrina was in her nineties. Among her fans, she was renowned for her fried chicken, among other things. But, by Willie Mae's own design, her restaurant was almost unknown around New Orleans, even in the black community. S. M. Hahn—the best writer in *The Times-Picayune*'s long line of restaurant critics—wrote the only known pre-Katrina full review of Willie Mae's. In it she described a sublime lunch. Then she said that its owner asked her not to identify the restaurant by name. So she didn't. I didn't recognize Hahn's description of the place, although I had visited Willie Mae's Scotch House a few times since the 1970s.

Like most other Mid-City restaurants, Willie Mae's sustained killing flood damage. Unlike any other, though, it became a cause celebre in the national media. John Currence, a James Beard award–winning restaurateur from Oxford, Mississippi, decided to move heaven and earth to get Willie Mae's back open again. He raised enough money and put in enough hours swinging a hammer to rebuild not only the restaurant but Willie Mae's house. He also raised enough consciousness about Willie Mae's that it won its own James Beard Foundation America's Classics Award in 2005.

Then, and only then, did people begin to call me on the air about Willie Mae's. The request was always the same: "Tell me about this

Willie Mae place. I never heard of it!" But to more than a few visiting journalists, it was the only restaurant in town. I think they were reading one another a bit too much, but that was pretty common. New Orleans eaters were proud and happy that Willie Mae and her restaurant received so much attention, even as many of them went there for the first time in their lives.

THE COMFORT OF FAMILIARITY

It's well known that people who survive a disaster grasp for whatever reminds them of their world as it was. Even for things they didn't particularly enjoy before. That's what happened to most New Orleanians, and it's one of the reasons that restaurants enjoyed such a spectacular renaissance after Katrina. With very few exceptions, they recognized that their customers needed the familiar, and they gave it to them.

The idea that people wanted only cliché comfort food proved to be a fallacy right away. The customers set restaurants straight about that. Soon enough the steaks, seafood, and poultry were once again napped with sauces and topped with clever garnishes.

What didn't come back, though, was the trendy food-magazine, television-chef food that had been on the verge of taking over before the storm. In its place was more unambiguously Creole and Cajun food than had been served in some time. We even saw the revival of many dishes from the old interchangeable menu days. Oysters Bienville and its kin, little seen for two decades outside the likes of Galatoire's and Antoine's, became proud specialties of chefs who might never have eaten—let alone cooked—them before.

Even the most avant-garde chefs embraced familiarity. Slade and Allison Rushing, young chefs who were married to each other (chef couples were a curious new phenomenon after the storm) even developed a new approach to oysters Rockefeller. In their post-Katrina restaurants Longbranch and MiLa, they deconstructed the dish. Here were the oysters, there was the spinach, the bits of licorice root (replacing the similar flavor of fennel), and the butter drizzled all over. Didn't look like oysters Rockefeller; didn't taste like them, either. But you could catch their drift, and it rang at least a faint bell with the homesick diners of New Orleans. It became the Rushings' signature dish. They were leaning pretty far over the water with that one, but at least they were doing it from a familiar boat.

Most of the reinforcement of Creole flavors came from the neighborhood restaurants, though. Their numbers increased at an accelerating rate following the hurricane, throughout even the most damaged parts of the city. Ironically, one of the reasons the neighborhood cafés did so well was that the chain restaurants took their good old time about reopening. Many of them never did. The customers they stole from the neighborhood cafés in the 1970s came back home. More people were eating more poor boy sandwiches than they had in decades. Better yet, they were getting excited about finding such great replacements for ordinary burgers. Whenever the subject of poor boys, fried seafood loaves, or muffulettas came up on the radio, it brought a swell of new callers, each of whom said they had found the best ones in town, in some place I had never heard of.

This gratified every red-blooded sleazy chic Orleanian and awakened some deeply buried instinct to go out there and find the good gumbo, stuffed mirliton, and fried chicken again. And they did.

It amazed even overoptimistic me. For example, in the years right before the storm, a terrific cluster of little restaurants grew up around the corner of Canal and Carrollton, the center of Mid-City. During the storm, between six and eight feet of floodwater flowed there, and it took more than two weeks to flow out. Everything was wrecked. The traffic signal at that busy intersection didn't function for eight months. It was a bad place to go if you didn't like being in collisions.

Suddenly, a block away, Angelo Brocato's Italian Ice Cream Parlor was having a street party, celebrating not only its return to business, but the one hundredth anniversary it missed because of the storm. It seemed only a few days later that all the other restaurant spaces were busy again—if not with their prestorm occupants, then with new ones. The neighborhood had such a buzz that one restaurant—Doson's Noodle House, a Vietnamese café—moved there from an unflooded location, even though it meant having to perform an expensive repair of the deeply flooded new premises.

The signal event in the renaissance of the Canal-Carrollton neighborhood was the legendary neighborhood restaurant Mandina's. When it reopened in the great old building that the owners at first thought would have to come down, it brightened the hearts of people who had never even dined there. Just knowing that you could sit down to Mandina's shrimp rémoulade, turtle soup, and soft-shell crabs amandine made living in the still lightly inhabited Mid-City neighborhood a rational proposition. It had the same effect on other neighborhoods, as well.

The most-covered story about post-Katrina ethnic dining in New Orleans involved the large number of Hispanic workers who came to help with rebuilding houses and other needed work. It wasn't long after the hurricane before taco trucks appeared on street corners. Those who'd enjoyed them in Houston and on the West Coast were primed for this new addition to the scene. Unfortunately, the taco trucks never really caught on before they were legislated out of town. Some of their owners stayed on to open permanent restaurants. They added to the sparse local community of Mexican and Central American restaurants, but not as much as many people had hoped for. I think this welcome development will take hold, but it will take a few more years.

PART FIVE

The Next Course

The cover of an early issue of *The New Orleans Menu* magazine, from 1982. *Menu* has since evolved into a daily online newsletter at www.nomenu.com.

CHAPTER THIRTEEN

Standing Reservations

THE WORLD COMES BACK

I wonder how Charles Dow and Edward Jones felt about the fame of their widely quoted stock average. It's a cut-and-dried number, the result of a rote calculation. But it's mentioned constantly in every news medium around the world. Even people who never heard of their much greater creation—*The Wall Street Journal*—know what the Dow Jones Industrial Average is.

I never would have guessed that my list of open restaurants, topped by the number of entries in it, would bring more attention than anything else in my journalistic career. Anyone could have done it. My New Orleans Restaurant Index gave only the name, address, phone number, and cuisine of all the restaurants that managed to resume service after Hurricane Katrina. No need for writing talent, discerning taste, or an expense account. Just a phone and the ability to count.

Suddenly, people and institutions who never heard of *The New Orleans Menu* started checking its restaurant list daily. The number of open restaurants became a widely quoted datum, a vital sign of the recovery in New Orleans. The mayor and other public officials mentioned it in speeches and interviews. It brought so much attention to my Web site that subscriptions to it tripled in less than a year.

I will brag that my list gave the clearest picture of the state of the dining scene of all the available statistics. The Louisiana Restaurant Association had a list, too, but it was based on the state's Department of Health's inspections. Not all the restaurants that passed the inspection were actually open. And the LRA's list included many food services that few people would consider restaurants. Hospital kitchens, gas stations serving hot dogs and Icees, and pizza delivery outfits were in there. Coffee shops that cooked nothing on-site. School cafeterias. Are those restaurants? I wouldn't say so.

I wouldn't bring this up except that the LRA's numbers showed a much lower percentage of restoration of the dining scene than my survey of real restaurants did. Why they disseminated the numbers to the media is something I'll never understand. National reporters dropping in for a few days to have some of Willie Mae's great chicken and take yet another look at the razed Lower Ninth Ward also had a way of grabbing the LRA's unnecessarily pessimistic numbers, while the real story about the New Orleans food scene was demonstrably much brighter.

Most people who don't live in New Orleans (and many who do) don't understand that the function of cooking and eating for us goes far beyond just passing time and allaying hunger. For New Orleans people, food is an extraordinarily large facet of life. You'd have to go to Italy or France or China to find that passion as intense as it is in Southeast Louisiana.

New Orleans is one of the few places in America where lustily enjoyable food is found in the homes and restaurants of the entire population, from those who have to rely on relief to the very wealthy. Not only do the poor not eat especially poorly here, but they eat a lot of the same things that the rich do. A graph of all the people who eat red beans and rice on a given Monday would show a more or less straight, horizontal line across the income axis. Same for gumbo on Friday. Fried chicken at Mardi Gras. Poor boys at lunchtime. Boiled crawfish in April. And so it goes.

There's little difference between the food eaten by black and white New Orleanians either. I discovered that when I first ventured into black-owned restaurants early in the 1970s. I don't know what I expected, but it wasn't that Eddie Baquet's gumbo would taste exactly like the gumbo my mother made. That happened again when I had roast chicken at Dooky Chase and red beans at Dunbar's. Coming at this from the other direction, only rarely have I had better oysters Bienville and Rockefeller than the ones from chef Austin Leslie's famed soul-food kitchen at Chez Helene.

There's nothing surprising about any of this. New Orleanians of African descent contributed at least as much to Creole cooking as any other source did. Until chef Paul Prudhomme made the profession of cooking cool for young people of all backgrounds, black cooks owned the kitchens of most New Orleans restaurants.

Of course, people from any heritage who earn better-than-average incomes spend more for their food, and because of that they eat more expensive foodstuffs. There is no known backstreet recipe for foie gras. But using food of advanced pedigree doesn't guarantee a better-tasting dish. It's accepted local gospel that the best versions of many indispensable, favorite New Orleans dishes are more likely to be found in the inexpensive joints than the gourmet palaces. It's not a forgone conclusion that the fried oysters at Commander's Palace are better than the ones at Bozo's (cf. "sleazy chic").

What this all added up to—and what my restaurant index proved—was that New Orleans could not survive unless its native food culture was saved first. The passion for food here is integral. Pandemic. Indispensable. Like breathing. As if we were on an airplane during an emergency, we needed to don our oxygen masks before helping others—you can't help anybody if you pass out.

The uniformity of goodness found from the bottom of New Orleans to the top misled many visiting journalists. They kept insisting that the grassroots sources of Creole cuisine must surely be dead after Katrina. They looked for struggling cafés, and found them, of course. (They were always around, no more so after than before the storm.) Then they filled in the details of an a priori conclusion, at which their minds arrived even before their bodies landed at Louis Armstrong International Airport.

Some national coverage of the recovery went beyond one-dimensional to downright infuriating. Certain editorials in newspapers around the country asked whether New Orleans shouldn't, really, be abandoned to the unconquerable elements, and its citizens forced to move elsewhere. One particularly strong call came from the usually mellow *National Geographic*. For the most part, we laughed at such conclusions as the thinking of people who had no idea how pleasurable it is to live here.

Alan Richman, *GQ*'s restaurant critic, wrote an article that was emphatically not funny. He came to New Orleans less than a year after the hurricane and asked, "As New Orleans struggles to bring the city and the tourists back, it's turning more and more to the food that made it famous. Can food save New Orleans?"

Not only can it, I would have told him, but it already had. But although he knows me quite well (we'd been on a couple of media trips together), he didn't ask. "I've never had much luck eating in New Orleans," he began. "I might be the only person who disliked Uglesich's." Aah. He didn't grok Creole *or* sleazy chic. He went on to apply New York City standards to our recovering restaurants. He found them wanting.

A lot of my listeners heard about (but few actually read) this article, and they called me on the air to discuss it. Why would a writer come here so soon after the worst natural disaster in American history and vent spleen because our restaurants weren't quite back up to world-class?

The *GQ* slight had no lasting effect. (New Orleans is unambiguously not a *GQ* kind of place.) But fuming about the article did get me thinking about what tone I should take in my own writing about the city's restaurants. I cut a lot of slack during the first months after the hurricane. How could I not? You can't insist that a person who just survived a bullet to the chest get right back to heavy lifting. It was clear to me that my role in the recovery of my city was to report on the progress of the culinary renaissance. That was not a made-up story, nor a puff job. The restaurants faced an extraordinary challenge and for the most part met it heroically.

I managed to talk a few journalists into that more optimistic (and, I would say, more accurate) perspective. The best result came from the producers of Anthony Bourdain's *No Reservations* on the Travel Network. They came to town in early 2008 to do an entire show on the recovery of New Orleans and its attractions. As usual, their first concern was the allegedly struggling corner joints. I told them that such a story had been done to death and wasn't an issue anyway, since by then we had more neighborhood restaurants open than we did before the hurricane. The better story—the one that almost nobody had touched—was about the big old restaurants, whose fight for life had been far more difficult. Specifically, I suggested they report the travails of Antoine's. They went along with it, and asked me to join in.

The shoot began, however, in the usual place: the Lower Ninth Ward. But that worked, because many of Antoine's employees had lived in that general area. (The real reason the producers liked it, though, was for the vivid visual drama of that wiped-out neighborhood.) Then we went to Antoine's. I gave Bourdain (who in person is exactly the guy you see on his Travel Channel show) a tour of the restaurant. I showed him where the walls and ceiling came close to caving in when the oldest of Antoine's buildings got hit by that minitornado, or whatever it was. Then we had lunch on-camera in the Last 1840 Room, a tiny red-walled private dining room tucked in next to the wine cellar. (Paul McIlhenny, the chairman of Tabasco, has adopted the Last 1840 as his personal dining room at Antoine's.)

Bourdain and I began with three rounds of Sazeracs. Then oysters Rockefeller, soft-shell crabs with brown butter, tournedos marchand de vin, and baked Alaska. A textbook meal at Antoine's, in other words. "Baked Alaska!" Bourdain said with incredulity when the football-size, meringue-fluffy mound of ice cream appeared. "So, let me see if I have this right. These guys are serving oysters Rockefeller and baked Alaska, not as an ironic menu statement, but for real?"

Of course. Why not? I said. This was Antoine's authentic food and had been for a century. Antoine's invented oysters Rockefeller. It's history, not irony. Like listening to Beethoven. What's wrong with keeping this unique, homegrown cuisine alive? Why would it be any less (or more) important than preserving the backstreet joints and their own style of Creole cuisine?

Tony Bourdain wasn't strong on the Antoine's storyline. His team also shot some other places around town, most of which were solidly sleazy chic. The shots of Antoine's—other than those showing Bourdain and me getting smashed on Sazeracs and scarfing soft-shell crabs—showed empty dining rooms. They said nothing about the fact that we were there at a time when the restaurant wasn't open, but never mind. The show did manage to illustrate the fix Antoine's and other grand old restaurants were in at the time; it was almost the first time that story had been told. It also showed that one could dress up and dine grandly in New Orleans again. No pestilence still raged. And that it was okay for lovers of the city to come back and enjoy themselves.

As We Are and Ever Shall Be

I resumed my restaurant reviews after only a few weeks' interruption. At first, these mainly reported how a restaurant had survived the ordeal, and what was on offer. It wasn't until six months after the hurricane that I began posting my star ratings on the reviews again. It was the only time I ever published reviews without them. Ratings are essential, I think, because they're unambiguous and make opinions easily comparable. I was the only critic in town who gave restaurant ratings during the next three years. For unknown reasons, *The Times-Picayune* didn't run restaurant reviews at all during that time.

Still, there's no question that I was more forgiving in my ratings after the storm than before. Or that many restaurants relied on sympathy to get away with less stringent standards.

I've since begun demanding better performance for my stars. I must. The rest of America continues to improve its tastes, expand its interest in food, and insist on better restaurants. As late as the 1970s New Orleans was one of only two or three American cities with numerous great restaurants, but that is no longer the case. We can't stand solely on our reputation or even our inimitable local cuisine. The most important force pushing the restaurants to move ahead is the knowledgeable local customer. My job is to needle both them and the restaurants, so they won't get complacent.

Restaurateurs, logically enough, are not especially fond of restaurant critics. At any given time, a few dozen restaurateurs are angry with me because of something I've said. Even good friends like chef Andrea get miffed now and then. That's as it should be. If you're going to be a serious, frank restaurant critic, a certain number of people unavoidably conclude you're some kind of pompous jerk. I can't say I like knowing that. But given the pleasures my strange occupation has brought me, I think I can live with it.

It had been my hope that by the fourth anniversary of the storm, in 2009, for the most part New Orleans could consider the Katrina disaster a thing of the past. My count of New Orleans restaurants of interest passed a thousand in the spring of 2009—for the first time in history. Even in the face of the recession that began in 2007, that and every other index of the culinary vitality of city continues to expand. The percentage of restaurant closings in New Orleans remains far lower than in other major cities.

There have even been new festivals, some of them impressively large. One of the most surprising is the Tales of the Cocktail, founded by Ann Tuennerman a few years before the hurricane. It has exploded into a major summertime event, going on for days with seminars, tastings, dinners, and music. It takes full advantage of the reborn popularity of cocktail drinking, and New Orleans's legitimate claim to having been the birthplace of the cocktail.

I had another optimistic hunch in the months after the storm. I predicted, in print, that by the end of 2008, the New Orleans metropolitan area would have as many people as it did before the hurricane. The actual figure from the U.S. Census Bureau came in at around 86 percent, although recent data seem to indicate that number should be revised upward. Of this there is no doubt: The area's population is still increasing. People who thought they would never return have continued to trickle back in. All that is much better than most predictions made in the year after Katrina.

Those who do return can be reassured by what has been done to repair and strengthen the New Orleans drainage system. The calamitous flooding was almost entirely the fault of a plan devised more than a century ago, when few people lived in the parts of the city that flooded after Katrina. The drainage canals carried water for three miles through those areas, at the same height as the lake's water. All the broken levees were on those canals, which in 2005 ran through densely populated areas. New floodgates allow those canals to be closed, preventing the water in them from getting so high. New pumping stations are at the lake's edge, where they belong, instead of in the center of town. That last improvement should have been carried out in the 1930s, when the lowest parts of the city were built up. If it had, Katrina would not have been a tenth of the disaster it was.

On the other hand, it would take a Pollyanna to ignore the ongoing storm-related problems. Most of them are concentrated in the neighborhoods that went deepest underwater. The housing stock of the city is still in very bad shape. As of 2009, at least 70,000 houses (estimates vary) that existed before the storm are either uninhabitable, vacant, or have been demolished. Many square miles of formerly solid neighborhoods remain only sparsely resettled. The people who once lived there but returned are mostly in the suburbs now and will likely remain there. The worst-devastated sections, meanwhile, wait to be the new neighborhoods of the future.

Except for the drainage system, the infrastructure of Orleans Parish is in terrible condition. It will take decades to repair, and that's with luck. To pick on something obvious, the streets of the city are still hard to negotiate. Driving through Lakeview and Gentilly, and other sections where the weight of the floodwater buckled the streets, is hazardous at any speed. Even St. Charles Avenue—the grand avenue of New Orleans, with its stateliest mansions and grandest live oaks—is in appalling condition for such an important tourism draw. The best way to travel it is to take the streetcar, which was there before the road was. Even that took more than three years to fix, while New Orleanians' hearts panged for the return of the 1923-vintage cars on the world's longest-running street railway.

And then there is the crime. While most of the frightening statistics tell of poor-on-poor crimes in remote parts of town, murders on the Mardi Gras parade routes and in the French Quarter happen with too much frequency not to generate alarm among visitors. (All of it, of course, is equally bad.)

For that and other reasons (the downturn in the national economy was no bonus), tourism is still nowhere near what it was before the hurricane. And tourism is the city's top moneymaker. It certainly is a critical support for the local restaurant industry. The off-season, from late July through September, has become even slower than it already was. On the other hand, June and December have become much better.

So New Orleans has a smaller population and fewer visitors than before the storm. But more restaurants! How have they all survived? The citizens needed them to offset the distress in other parts of their lives. The restaurants, little and big, offer a familiar escape, a method of restoring smiles to faces and optimism to outlooks.

The recovery of the eating scene benefited me more than most people. It's often said that most people eat to live, but that New Orleans people live to eat. As for me, I eat for a living. And the living has been embarrassingly good. New Orleanians apparently enjoy talk about food as much as they do the food itself, and food talk is what I sell. My cookbook, *Tom Fitzmorris's New Orleans Food*, came out in March 2006, and it has done well. It dramatically increased the number of cooking questions I get on the radio, for one thing, thereby selling still more copies.

The New Orleans Menu Daily grew tremendously after the hurricane, and now has about 10,000 subscribers, from all over the place. I write between 4,000 and 5,000 words every weekday for it, including a comprehensive restaurant review, a recipe or two, a list of the best of this or that, an almanac of food events, and a short and controversial piece of serial fiction. The most popular part of the newsletter is my Dining Diary, a journal I began to publish in 1996—years before the word *blog* came into existence. I've always larded the journal heavily with deeply personal stuff, which readers tell me is their favorite part. I don't understand why, but I'm happy about it.

Meanwhile, my radio show is now into its third decade. It continues to defy radio conventions: Everything on the station now is sports—except for those three daily hours of *The Food Show*. And the Eat Club dinners keep filling with fifty or so people every week.

FIXING A HOLE

Katrina's floodwater stopped at the first step of the New Orleans Fairmont Hotel. But the hotel could just as well have been in the ten-foot-deep zone. With all its utilities in the basement, the hotel suffered such damage, and its reopening required such an enormous investment in reconstruction, that the Fairmont management and the hotel's owners essentially walked away. The hotel sat empty and rotting for years.

This opened a pit in the hearts of many New Orleanians. The Roosevelt (that was the hotel's name during most of its 110-year history) had been indisputably the city's leading hotel. It was the place where people had the grandest dinner dates, held their wedding receptions, and brought their kids every Christmas to marvel at the spectacular displays in the magnificent lobby. Famous people and politicians stayed there, often making headlines while doing so. Its restaurant set the local standard for elaborateness and excellence. Its catering department mounted the most impressive wine dinners imaginable, in the days when only members of gourmet societies went to such things. And then there was the Blue Room, a formal nightclub with its own big band and headline acts whose names you'd immediately recognize. The Blue Room broadcast its shows on CBS Radio nationwide every night for almost forty years.

And then Katrina reduced this wonderful machine of happiness to a dark, dead, moldy hulk. Nothing happened. No word was heard that anything *would* happen. There it squatted, in a highly visible spot just off Canal Street, extending a full block, depressing everybody and everything around it. It was never hard to find ways of darkening one's mood in the years after Katrina, but that one was a downer of unique proportion.

The turnaround was so sudden that we were all caught by surprise when, in June 2009, the hotel emerged from an accelerated renovation and reopened. Under the management of the auspicious Waldorf-Astoria hotel group, yet. It is once again the Roosevelt (many New Orleanians never stopped calling it that, even after thirty years as the Fairmont). It's not as big as it had been (which was enormous), but nothing suggests that a blight came through.

The lobby is still a block long. Right off it is the Sazerac Bar, named for the concoction of rye whiskey, anise liqueur, and bitters that lays claim to being the world's first cocktail (the one invented in New Orleans in the late 1700s). Next door is the Sazerac Restaurant, not as grand as in the days of full tableside service, but a close approximation, with contemporary, less formal codes of dress and service.

The gourmet restaurant in the reborn Roosevelt is Domenica. The name is Italian for Sunday, the day when locals were most likely to have been seen in the Roosevelt during its prime. The food is Italian, too. It's the sixth restaurant under the aegis of chef John Besh, all of them quite substantial, no two alike. With Domenica, Besh—easily the hottest of post-Katrina chefs—now has twice as many New

Orleans restaurants as does Emeril. Or any of the branches of the Brennan family.

Clearly, here was a new life force in New Orleans. At the time of Katrina, Besh's sole establishment was Restaurant August. That was the restaurant I thought I saw burning in the background when, martini in hand, perched on the edge of a sofa in Atlanta, I watched Anderson Cooper's satellite-phone report three days after Katrina. August was also the restaurant where, a few days after I returned from evacuation, the much delayed, crisis-level service of an abbreviated but well-cooked dinner made me believe that, in New Orleans, our food would heal us.

I haven't since seen or heard from the people who invited me to that revelatory, relieved meal. I think I'll track them down and have another dinner with them and John Besh, at Domenica. We reunited strangers will exchange the Katrina hug, then we will eat well.

ACKNOWLEDGMENTS

A Toast

I'll make this short so more people will read it. This book was initiated by Leslie Stoker of Stewart, Tabori & Chang during a dinner we shared at Antoine's in 2008. The book she had in mind was quite a bit different from the one I sent in. By the time I replaced a number of chapters and reworked the others with Leslie's perspective in mind, we had a much better work. I thank her for her vision and understanding.

I also credit fellow food writer Amy Wilensky, who performed much of the editing, manicuring the briars that have a way of entangling my writing and thinking. Her insights make the reading more agreeable and elegant, without blunting its points.

Writing and the other ways I spend my time are no longer of the tiniest interest to my teenage children Jude and Mary Leigh. But I've never thanked them in public for putting up with my not-so-family-friendly career. They understood why Daddy was eating in restaurants every evening instead of doing the things a more conventionally employed dad does with his kids. Their creativity in thinking up alternative ways for us to spend rich times together brought me more happiness than any person has a right to expect. And I'm speechlessly proud of what they've done with their lives.

By pulling countless things together for me in the last twenty years, Mary Ann Connell is also responsible for making this book possible. She hired me for my big radio gig, became my wife, gave our children the ultimate in mothering, and showed me strategies for living I never would have discovered on my own. Meanwhile, she let me pursue my passion for food, even though she thinks I grossly overestimate its importance. I love her for (as she would say) giving me a life.

INDEX